Truman of St. Helens

Truman
of St. Helens

THE MAN AND HIS MOUNTAIN

Shirley Rosen

Warmest wishes,
Shirley Rosen

MADRONA PUBLISHERS   •   Seattle

LONGVIEW PUBLISHING CO.   Longview

10 9 8 7 6 5 4 3 2

Library of Congress Cataloging in Publication Data

Rosen, Shirley.
   Truman of St. Helens : the man and his mountain.

   1. Truman, Harry, 1896-1980.   2. Hotelkeepers—
Washington (State)—Biography.   3.. Saint Helens,
Mount (Wash.)   I. Title.
TX910.5.T78R67 1981   979.7'84033   81-4304
ISBN 0-914842-57-9   AACR2

Madrona Publishers
2116 Western Avenue
Seattle, Washington 98121

For Wayne McGuire who said, "You can do it."
And to those special teachers everywhere who give
their students the courage to try.

And

For the memory of Auntie Eddie, who once said,
"Truman, some day they're going to write a book
about you."

And

With love to my mom, Esther Burke, who joined
Auntie Eddie and Truman on March 22, 1981.

Acknowledgments

To my editor John Marshall, who made this into a book I can be really proud of; who took 450 pages of manuscript and with his talented pen and scissors cut, rearranged and shaped the material to 220 pages. His dedication to the project from beginning to end is something I will always appreciate.

To my husband Lee for not disowning me during the time I wrote this book, while he put up with supermarket traffic jams, washed clothes, spent hours learning to cook, and listened to a clacking typewriter until the wee hours of the morning. To our son Chris, who kept saying, "Mom, when are you going to finish?" To our daughter Teresa, who worried about her dad, and to our son Keith, who was the first person to encourage me to write a book.

To the rest of my family: my sister Dayle Gorringe for her phenomenal memory, encouragement and support in the creation of the book; my mom Esther Burke for her recollections; and my sister Elaine Mount, who sent me her Truman notes. To my cousins Carolyn Hibler and Kathy Rohrbach.

To my publishers: in particular Sam Angeloff of Longview Publishing, who felt this was a pretty good yarn and helped me weld it into the final revision; John M.

McClelland, Jr., who had faith in the project; and Dan Levant of Madrona who said yes and felt Truman's life was worth telling.

To the staff at the Shoreline Community College Library, who never failed me, and to Wayne McGuire and Denzil Walters of the college English department for their encouragement.

To Joyce Barnum, Reference Librarian at the Suzzallo Library of the University of Washington, who dug deep for information on Truman's World War I aero squadron. To Steve Malone, seismologist at the University of Washington who verified the eruptive phases of Mount St. Helens for me.

To my friend Sarah Blumenthal who transcribed hours of tapes. To the Dahlbergs and Wintons who let me use their quiet homes while they were on vacation. To my neighbor and friend Dick Barrett who read and laughed at what I wrote.

Most of all, tons of appreciation and thanks to Truman's friends—all 110 of you—who shared a part of your lives with me and taught me so much about the man beneath the salty surface. I couldn't have written this without you. I regret that not all of you and all of your anecdotes could be in the book, but the publisher felt a 700-page book was too long.

To all of you who generously gave me slides and photographs: George Barker for the cover picture, George Bowers, Art and Nadine Clarkson, Cathleen Douglas for directing me to Justice Douglas's private collection at the Yakima Valley Museum, Karen Jacobsen, Joan Leonard, Jim, Pauline and Margaret Lund, James McCoy, Dude Mullooly, Gunnar Nilsson, Mary Lou and Rob Quoidbach, Chuck Tonn, Rex and Ruth West, and Vicki Weiss.

To Jesse Riffe for his 1918 postcard from Truman, to Ted and Emma Landes for their 1918 newspaper articles, and to Marjorie Aldrich for sharing *Memories from Family Albums,* her book about early days in east Lewis County. To N. B.

Gardner and to Margaret, the lovely lady Mount Margaret was named for, both of whom filled me in on the early history of the Mount St. Helens area.

To Carl Berg and Fred Stocker for giving me their very special Truman tapes.

To Truman, who was always present while I wrote about his life, and to all the people in the book who are no longer alive.

Contents

1: Twenty-four Hour Encounter   1

2: Tumbling Memories   17

3: Early Times   28

4: War and Prohibition   37

5: Building Years   45

6: War and Peace   54

7: A Diary and a Distinguished Visitor   61

8: Best Friends   85

9: Sudden Death   107

10: Under the Volcano   126

11: Tracking Down Truman   150

Illustrations: follow page 52

1: Twenty-four Hour Encounter

AT 8:32 A.M., Sunday, May 18, 1980, Mount St. Helens in Washington State erupted with the explosive force of 10 million tons of TNT. I first heard the news in a telephone call from my sister and my immediate thoughts were of my 83-year-old uncle, Harry Truman, who owned a 50-acre resort on the shores of Spirit Lake. Harry was his given name, but if anyone asked he'd say, "Just call me Truman."

I feared for his safety because he was in a direct line with the north slope of the mountain and less than three miles from the site of the explosion. He had lived there 54 years, and vowed he would never leave his home, despite warnings of the impending eruption.

As I sat and stared out the living room window of my Seattle home, my mind was flooded with memories. They wandered back to the summer of 1948 when I was fourteen and that first day I had worked for my aunt and uncle at Mount St. Helens Lodge.

That first quiet night was so clear I felt I could easily reach up and touch the stars. I was exhausted, and I tumbled into the large, soft double bed upstairs in the main lodge and quickly fell asleep.

Just as quickly, I was jarred awake by a raspy bellowing. "Goddamn son-of-a-bitch, get the hell out of here." The voice was Truman's, and it came from outside, two floors below. I slipped out of my cozy bed, and my bare feet

1

shuddered from the cold wooden floor. In the passageway below, ominous lights reflected on the walls in the maze of corridors.

As I approached the window at the landing of the long stairway to the main floor of the lodge, Truman's bellowing became louder. Then I could see him, outside, bamboo rake in hand, clad only in his Jockey shorts. He was using the rake to beat the backside of a black bear, which was gorging himself on the remains of Auntie Eddie's delicious trout dinner. Large paws clawed through the trash strewn out of the garbage cans the bear had toppled. The bear paid no attention to Truman's whacking as splintered shafts of the rake flew around the parking lot.

I suppressed my urge to laugh because I also felt fear as I watched Truman as he battered and cursed the bear. Then the bear's gluttonous sounds became a rumbling growl, and suddenly, he whirled. He reared up on his hind legs and his black shaggy head swayed from side to side. The moonlight shone on Truman's face and I could see his shock as he realized the bear was twice his height—and angry now. With a mammoth paw, the bear took a swipe at Truman and just missed. In the chase that followed, Truman looked like a character from an old Charlie Chaplin movie as he zig-zagged across the parking lot at twice his normal speed. The bear loped after him and took another swipe. The bear seemed to move in slow motion, but his strides were long, and he was amazingly fast.

Truman deftly calculated the distance to the door of the basement where he kept a large array of hunting guns. He shifted his pace, rotating until his back was to the door. He flew through, quickly grabbed a gun, loaded it, and fired at the bear. The bear turned and galloped off as the sound of the gunshot died away.

I quickly made my way back up to my third-floor room and peeked out the tiny wood-frame window above my bed. I saw flickers of light dance in the night down the lane of cabins as people lit their kerosene lanterns. Then one by one, the flickers of light gradually disappeared. I saw Spirit Lake shimmering through the trees in front of the cabins as the tranquil quiet returned. I slipped back under the covers and could hear the murmur of Auntie Eddie and Truman discussing the bear escapade in their quarters below. I fell asleep with the image of Truman in his underwear retreating from the bear in the moonlight.

Early the next morning, I could hear Truman whistling a cheery tune outside as he went about his preparations for the weekend customers. I would become accustomed to that whistling; it was my alarm and I immediately knew I'd better get up and get cracking because there was work to be done, even though the small clock on the nightstand beside my bed would invariably read 6:00 A.M.

I figured I had five to ten minutes to get dressed while Truman was walking to unlock the single gas pump. It was old, 10 feet tall, with a glass cylinder on top, which was covered with wire mesh. People were always asking Truman if they could buy some gas, but he'd always tell them, "No...go down the road a piece, maybe they'll sell you some, this is for my own use." Then he'd turn and say, "Stupid sons-a-bitches, you'd think they'd knowed better than to come 50 miles without a full tank of gas."

I dressed looking out the dormer window at the intense azure sky. I could see only a portion of Mount St. Helens—the dense forest across the road blocked the rest. To the right of the blacktop, I could see the clear water of the Toutle River where it began gurgling its way toward Castle Rock.

I walked down the stairway to the spacious main room of the lodge. The old oak crank telephone on the wall, the communication link with the boat dock 150 yards away, was jingling. I answered. Red Hiles, who Truman hired away from Gustafson's Spirit Lake Lodge five years before, said the customers in cabin 12 should be charged $5 for their two-hour use of an outboard motorboat. They had caught six rainbow trout during their dawn fishing excursion.

I walked to the kitchen which spanned the lodge from front to back. It was about 15 feet wide and had eye-level windows that gave a good view of the cars driving up the highway.

Auntie Eddie was putting cream on her face in front of a small mirror perched on the window sill. She smiled broadly at me and asked what I wanted for breakfast. Her long tapered fingers wiped the slippery substance from her face, with its soft rosy complexion which came from her Swedish ancestry. She stood straight and seemed taller to me than her five-foot-five-inch height.

After applying bright red lipstick, Auntie Eddie walked to the gas stove where a pan was simmering. Cow brains, she explained matter-of-factly. She poured off the hot water and gingerly placed the brains on the breadboard next to the kitchen sink. Removing the thin membrane was a tedious task, but one Auntie Eddie enjoyed because brains were Truman's favorite breakfast. He enjoyed the way she would finely chop the brains to just the right consistency and then would scramble in three eggs, carefully folding the two ingredients together. The aroma of butter filled the air as it sizzled in the frying pan.

Truman came up the back stairs banging his feet as he always did, to release the dirt from his boots. His large hands smoothed down his thinning sandy brown hair as he entered the kitchen and said, "Hi kid." Walking to the stove, he leaned down and rested his chin on Auntie Eddie's shoulder, patting her bottom as he peered over to see what she was cooking. Then he danced a little step sideways to the sink where he washed his hands with Boraxo. Looking like a gleeful little boy, he slid a small paint-worn stool out from under the low work counter of the old-fashioned kitchen cupboard where we all sat and ate our meals.

He poured a glass of buttermilk, picked up the pepper shaker and tapped it with his little finger until the surface of the buttermilk was sprinkled black. "This'll keep a man v-e-e-rile," he chortled. Then he took a long lingering drink

and sighed with pleasure as Auntie Eddie placed his breakfast in front of him. After eating all he could with a fork,
Truman broke a piece of toast in two and swabbed his plate
to capture every last morsel. He chug-a-lugged his second
glass of buttermilk and rubbed his slightly round stomach.
"No city folk and damn few country folk have ever ate like
this," he said. His tongue twirled across the mustache of
buttermilk on his upper lip, then he wiped away the re-
mainder with the back of his hand and let out a loud belch of
approval.

Truman snuck up behind Auntie Eddie and swatted her a
good one on the backside, his own special thank-you for
preparing his favorite breakfast. "Get your ass out of here
Truman," she said. He was 13 years her senior, but they
seemed just the same age.

Red had just come up from the boathouse and was pouring himself a cup of coffee. Truman placed his white yachting cap on the back of his head and walked to the kitchen
doorway, which was the entrance to the main floor of the
lodge. Next to the door was a large blackboard where the
rented cabin numbers were marked down. There was a
quick discussion concerning which cabins needed cleaning,
which ones were reserved and who would be staying over.
Truman was keenly aware of who his guests were and
whether they used boats. If they rented cabins, that was one
thing, but if they also rented his boats they got special
attention from him. The boats brought in more money.

Truman walked out toward the two front doors in the
main room, chattering all the while in his deep gravelly
voice. Then he quickly walked down the four cement steps
which surrounded the big front porch, and he was off —
arms swinging, still talking as he headed for the boathouse.

I put on an apron to get ready for the guests from upstairs
in the lodge and from a couple of the sleeping cabins who
would soon be coming for breakfast. Frank Wilkinson came
in, a retired railroad cook who had worked for Gustafson's
Spirit Lake Lodge until Truman had hired him away a

couple years before. Frank was warm, friendly, and fatherly. He put on his chef's hat over his graying hair and tied a big white apron around his large stomach. He'd drive up every morning in his old vintage car from his small cabin six miles down the Spirit Lake Highway, at Coldwater Creek. Frank mixed up enough pancake batter in a big stainless steel pitcher to last two days and usually used a quart of fresh buttermilk, which always irritated Truman. When the lush mountain huckleberries were ripe, we'd pick them out behind the lodge and Frank would sprinkle them on the homemade buttermilk pancakes before turning them over on the large griddle.

Auntie Eddie and I waited on tables while Frank cooked. There was a hole in the wall and an eye-level shelf between the kitchen and the main room, where we picked up orders Frank had prepared. There were two long counters in the main room and four booths against the wall at the front of the lodge.

I remember the first time I waited on a table. I was scared and shaking so much I thought I'd spill food all over. When I carried the two plates across the 40-foot dance floor, I felt it was quite an accomplishment. Then I turned around to go back to the kitchen and there were three laughing faces watching me. Auntie Eddie, Truman and Frank all thought it was pretty funny that I was so nervous—and by the end of the summer I thought it was, too.

The scent of fresh-brewed coffee hung in the air. Frank filled the one-gallon enamel coffee pot with water and a half-pound of coffee, then brought it to a boil. As he cooked eggs for breakfast orders, Frank would toss shells into the coffee, to settle the grounds. We transferred the coffee to a glass Silex pot and when we served it people always said, "That's the best coffee I've ever tasted."

Everyone who came in that morning asked what had happened the previous night. We casually dismissed their questioning: "Oh, Truman took a shot at a bear." But when Truman told the story, it was hilarious. He loved an audi-

ence and he explained every detail so fast that if you didn't
listen closely you'd miss half of what he was saying. His large
work-worn hands gestured as he spoke. "There I was running around in my underwear for the whole goddamn
world to see, with the moon shining on me like a goddamn
World War II spotlight, and that son-of-a-bitchin' bear had
me trapped. It was a big black bastard, and must of weighed
over 600 pounds. Had a white patch on his chest, he did. But
it'll take a lot more than an old black bastard bear to do ol'
Truman in. Singed his furry ass with a shot I did. It'll be a
cold day in hell before he gets guts enough to come that
close to my lodge again."

As quickly as Truman started the conversation, he
abruptly ended it. Then he took off in his brisk, half-
running walk, arms swinging at his sides. He had too much
energy to stay in one place for long.

After we washed breakfast dishes, we cleaned cabins. But
that first Friday, Truman came banging up the stairs to the
kitchen. "Okay, kid, come on," he said. "I want you to know
where in the hell you're at so you can answer questions when
someone asks. You'll get some of the most goddamn stupid
questions, but then you'll get some that aren't so stupid and
you should be able to answer them."

As we walked to the lake, he took a large white handker-
chief out of his pocket, spread it carefully across his right
hand, raised it to his face, and loudly blew his slightly
bulbous nose. Then he began his lesson:

"We're on the north side of the mountain, 46 miles east of
Castle Rock. If folks want groceries, we've got a few for sale
up in the lodge, but the closest store is down the road 27
miles in Kid Valley."

Truman seemed to enjoy sharing his knowledge with me
and wasn't in his usual rush as we stood at the base of a giant
tree. "Those redwoods down in California don't have anything on us," Truman said. "Look at that." He pointed up-
ward to the top of the 250-foot Douglas fir which was about
eight feet in diameter at shoulder level. Pulling out his

pocket knife, Truman cut a notch in the tree to show me the
thickness of the red-brown bark. "I've seen the Douglas
felled with bark a foot thick. Some are 300 years old."

The fragrance of pine and fir was pungent in the morning air. The new spring foliage erupted from branches of
the trees. "People are always askin' if that mountain's Mount
Rainier. That's a stupid goddamn question. St. Helens may
not be as big, but she's purtier than old Rainier and she's got
a beautiful lake right at her feet, too." He went on to talk
about the President's plan to rename the Columbia National
Forest for Gifford Pinchot, the first Chief of the U.S. Forest
Service. Truman added, "I like Harry Truman; he's a gutsy
ol' codger. Bet he'll go down in history as one of the greatest
goddamn presidents this country ever had."

The two Trumans reminded me of each other. Their
words were never fancy; they were never obscure, either. It
was never hard to figure out what either Truman was saying.
I didn't remember the President cussing quite as much as
my uncle did, but swearing just seemed to be a part of his
chatter. It was so constant you eventually didn't notice it at
all, except when he'd turn it off like he did when Grandma
Lund was present. Truman didn't seem too sure of himself when Eddie's mother was around.

We walked down to the floating boat dock, and Truman
explained that Spirit Lake was 3,200 feet above sea level,
two-and-one-half miles long, and had twelve miles of
shoreline. "I moved up here in 1926, not long after they
finished Coe's Dam, which raised the lake two feet," he said.
"If anyone asks you how deep the lake is, tell them the
bottom hasn't been found yet. That always gets them goin'."
(About two weeks later, Auntie Eddie heard me respond
to a customer's question about the depth of the lake and
burst out laughing. She didn't even correct me just then; I
said the bottom hadn't been found, and the people believed
me. But after the customers walked out of the lodge, she
told me the lake was 184 feet deep.)

The boat dock spanned the headwaters of the Toutle

River which was about 150 feet across. Our feet clunked on the planks and the sound echoed down the river. On one side of the float, there was a bench with a backrest where people could sit and view the lake, or turn around and look down river and up at the mountain. On the lake side of the float, there were boat slips. Twelve boats with five-horsepower motors were gassed and ready for rental. On the far side of the river was a boathouse where Truman kept the Chris Craft motor launch which he used for sightseeing tours around the lake. By the boathouse were 15 to 20 rowboats and six canoes upside down.

After explaining the rental fees to me, Truman turned abruptly and said, "Look at that! You'll never see anything more beautiful in the whole goddamn world than that old mountain. She's 9,677 feet tall. Captain George Vancouver discovered her in 1792 and he named her after Lord St. Helens, a British diplomat. The Indians called her 'Fire Mountain.' She erupted several times between 1842 and 1857 and is the youngest mountain in the Cascades. They say she's goin' to blow again and maybe soon, but they're lyin' like horses' trot. They don't know what the hell they're talkin' about. Look at her, she's not goin' no place." Truman's rugged face was radiant as he looked up at St. Helens. The perfectly symmetrical peak loomed over on us. The trees were dwarfed by it. I thought, "If I reach out, I bet I could pat the snow on her sides."

Truman's dog, Boy, nudged up for a pat and Truman bent over and slapped him affectionately. A taffy-brown chow and husky mix, Boy was always at Truman's side. Not far behind Boy we'd usually see Gilbert, a 25-pound salt-and-pepper gray cat with a big white chest, white paws in front and full white back legs. I had never seen such a big cat in my young life—and haven't since. That morning Gilbert had wandered down to the boat float and lay there basking in the sun as he watched the wild minks playfully jumping from log to log down the Toutle. They were about 50 feet from us. Truman explained the mink lived in tree trunks or old hollow logs near the edge of the river. Their soft fur was a glossy chestnut-brown and they had long bushy tails. They were gracefully diving in the water for fish. He told me what good hunters they were and how he liked having them around because they killed rats and mice.

Gilbert seemed to tire of their shenanigans and slowly got up, walking stealthily in their direction. Truman laughingly said, "Gilbert, you'd better watch out," as the cat started stalking the mink. He picked one out that was about two feet long and pounced on it. They fought fiercely, and I could see the mink dig its sharp teeth into Gilbert. There were yowling, crying noises. Truman stood there, excited like a man at a boxing match, slapping his hands together and yelling shouts of support at Gilbert. The mink was a light-weight in comparison, but suddenly flipped Gilbert five feet in the air. Gilbert took off like a shot, his tail between his legs, and was not seen for three days until Truman found him hiding in the basement. From that time on, Gilbert only had about half a left ear.

After we watched the fight, Truman told me to go on down the cabin lane to find Auntie Eddie so she could show me the routine of cleaning cabins. Cabin 12 had been va-cated and was the only one left that needed cleaning for the anticipated weekend business; it was right on the lake-front and had a sandy beach with a gradual incline.

Cabin 12 would become my favorite and we'd often swim there. But it was typical of most of the housekeeping cabins and accommodated four people. It had a porch across the front, bedrooms at either end, and in the center was a kitchen area with a wood stove and sink. Dishes were kept on open shelves. There was a good-sized kitchen table and two chairs. At that time there were no toilets in the cabins and no running water. There was a large galvanized bucket in the kitchen and a water spigot out in the cabin lane where people could draw fresh spring water. Each bedroom had a double bed, chair and kerosene lantern, as well as wash basin and towels. Auntie Eddie had everything color-coordinated in the cabins and spent winters making brightly colored curtains or mending sheets and spreads. There were curtains on wooden dowels, which could be pulled shut for privacy. There were linoleum floors, and brooms and cleaning supplies were furnished in the vain hope that people would clean up after themselves.

I can still smell the mixture of oil of wintergreen and kerosene we used as disinfectant. If we had to clean all the cabins in one day, it burned my nostrils and turned my hands raw. I vividly recall the cleaning routine Auntie Eddie taught me. Strip the beds and put the linen in the pillowcases; put them on the porch for Truman to pick up with the truck. Wash the dirty dishes and then scrub everything down with disinfectant. Check to make sure the cupboards and coolers were empty and make sure there was an adequate supply of wood, newspapers, and stick matches to start a fire. Wash the windows; sweep and wash the floor. Auntie Eddie even taught me how to miter sheets at the corners and to make a bed as smooth as glass.

Truman was always curious and wanted to know what was going on every place around the resort. No matter where we were or what we were doing, he'd show up. He'd poke his head in the door, and say, "How ya doin', girls?" Then he'd be off again on some task he had to accomplish. Later he'd come back and toss the soiled laundry into the back of his shiny maroon Chevrolet pickup truck. Auntie Eddie would climb in front and I'd hop on the tailgate.

Truman would stop at the two outhouses which were halfway between the cabins and lodge. "Go clean up after the dirty damned public," he'd say. "It smells like a goddamn whorehouse in there. I bet they wouldn't miss and piss all over their goddamn floors at home." I often wished I'd had a clothespin for my nose. I'd pour lye down the holes, wipe around them with the oil-of-wintergreen-kerosene mixture and sweep the floor. Sometimes I'd just mix up a bucket of disinfectant and slosh it all over. People would often come in the lodge and ask if they could use the indoor toilet because they didn't like to use the country outhouse. Truman would turn them away saying, "You're in God's country now, we don't have all those modern conveniences."

If people came in and asked for a drink of water, Truman would send them down to the spring, saying, "There's fresh spring water right by the Toutle. Just go down and drink all you want." Truman had built a dam high in the hill across the headwaters of the Toutle, and laid pipe downhill to the lodge. But the lines were frequently partly plugged, and the water pressure was so bad that we'd have to go down to the spring for water ourselves. Late in the summer the water level was so low that the trips to the spring were a daily occurrence. I can still feel the ice-cold water that sloshed out of the heavy galvanized buckets as I carried them the 100 yards to the lodge. I usually lost about half the water in the buckets before I got to the kitchen.

Truman's property bordered the Spirit Lake Campground which was a part of the National Forest Service. Jim Langdon, the District Ranger at Spirit Lake, was a good friend of Truman and before he retired, he made arrangements for Truman to tap into the Forest Service water supply. The fall of 1949 and spring of 1950 Truman ran water lines to the cabins and plumbed them for the guests. He put in septic tanks, and closed in a portion of the front porches where he installed toilets.

Truman had no use for people who stayed in the public campground. He'd say, "Those stupid goddamn squatters, they want to run an extension cord from their tent to one of my cabins so they can play their goddamn radio. Now just yesterday there was that lady who came in and wanted to know if she could use our washing machine to wash her baby's diapers and she proceeded to change the little bastard's shitty diapers right on the floor of the lobby and stunk the whole goddamn place up." He'd remember such an incident a week, a month, or even a year later and would say, "Those cheap sons-a-bitches steal me blind. I can't leave any of my tools out in plain sight. And they build those goddamn big bonfires and smog up the whole damn lake. They're the first to yell for being charged five dollars for a case of beer when they could have brought their own, and they yell even louder when we're out."

Sometimes, when it rained really hard, a family from the campground would come down the highway, walking in the door soaking wet. Truman would say, "Go on down the road a piece, maybe they've got a room. I'm full up." He wouldn't be, of course. They'd walk out dejectedly, and Truman would say, "Can't rent to them. They'd have the whole goddamn campground in one cabin before the night's over." He didn't have any love for pickup-mounted campers, either. I remember when he saw his first one, he sneered, "Now look at that, they're even bringing their own goddamn cabins with them."

That first day, we got back up to the lodge just in time to help Frank make sandwiches for the lunch trade. There wasn't a really large selection, but there were always generous fillings of ham, lunch meat, peanut butter or egg salad. Hot dogs were never served with a bun, but split and fried and then served as hot-dog sandwiches. Sandwiches cost 40 and 50 cents. Hamburgers were usually served on regular white bread because Truman would forget to buy hamburger buns. Potato chips were always served on the side with the sandwiches, along with bread-and-butter pickles.

Frank really enjoyed making pies. I watched in amazement as he worked, flipping the crust over, rolling it very thin, slipping it into the pie pans with the grace of an artist at work. His chubby hands moved quickly as he filled the waiting crusts with sliced apples, huckleberries or custard, which was Truman's favorite. But the most fun pie to watch him make was his famous mile-high pie he called Flough Dowdie. It took a dozen eggs for three pies, which he separated, beating until the whites were in tall peaks, then adding whipped cream and maraschino cherries.

When customers walked in the front door, I watched them halt and breathe deeply with pleasure when they

caught a whiff of Frank's pies. Whatever errand they may
have been on was soon forgotten. Saturdays and Sundays
people would drive up to the lake for the day, knowing after
a long ride they could get a piece of Frank's homemade pie.
Every stool at the two counters would be taken and all four
booths would be full. A piece of pie was 25 cents and coffee
was 10 cents a cup. Truman would sit down in his lounge
chair with a plate of custard pie perched on his left hand, his
mouth full, and say, "Ah, that's damn good pie, Frank."

That first afternoon, Truman told me, "Come on kid, I'm
goin' to teach you how to start the generator in the power
plant." "Who, me?" I asked. "Who else?" he snapped and my
lower lip began to tremble. I was afraid I wouldn't be able to
do it. "Think I'll call you 'Who Me,'" Truman laughed,
"You're always saying that when we tell you to do
something."

I followed him out to the power house where there were
two generators, which provided all of the resort's electricity.
The strong smell of oil and grease hit me as we walked in the
door of the small wood-frame structure. He said one engine
was the primary generator and the second one was an
auxiliary, in case the main generator failed. He patiently
explained how to prime the engine, and showed me how to
crank it, and how to let go of the handle before it could kick
me. I cranked and cranked until my shoulder ached. He
wasn't about to do it for me. He just said, "Crank it up, crank
it up." I remember how surprised I was when it finally
started. As we walked back to the lodge he slapped me on
the back saying, "Good job, 'Who Me.' See, that wasn't so
hard. Don't want you and Eddie to be without lights if Red
and I get stuck in town."

Late in the day Truman came up to the lodge and
plugged in all his beer signs. Even if he didn't carry a
particular brand of beer, he'd plug in the sign just for the
brightly colored lights. There was Rainier, Schlitz, Sicks
with a big number 66 at the window, Olympia, and a few
others. Truman didn't want to carry too many kinds of

beer. "Damn stupid public can't make up their minds if you give 'em too many choices," he'd say. "It just confuses 'em."

I never saw Truman drink much beer, but along about 4:00 or 5:00 each afternoon, he'd come in and say, "It's cocktail time." He'd take down his large old-fashioned Coca Cola glass, almost fill it with Coke, toss in a splash of Schenley's whiskey, drop in the ice cubes, and the drink invariably would slosh over onto the counter. The ice would crackle as frosty cubes hit the warm pop. Truman would take a big swig, breathe a deep sigh and say, "Ahhh, that's damn good Panther Pee."

"Now let's play a quick little ditty," he'd say, and trip the switch in the back of the nickelodeon. The first song he always played was "Bubbles in the Wine" by Lawrence Welk. On dark dreary mornings at about 6:30 A.M., he'd sometimes start up the generator, plug in all the beer signs and the nickelodeon, and turn the volume up so loud that the sound vibration from "Bubbles in the Wine" would almost knock me out of my bed on the third floor.

Dinner was always pretty much the same. There were usually two entrees—roast beef or roast pork—plus browned potatoes and some type of vegetable. There was seldom salad because it was difficult to keep produce fresh. With the dinner we served some homemade soup and fresh mountain huckleberry deep-dish cobbler or pie for dessert. Dinner cost $2.50.

We would no sooner finish washing the dinner dishes than the beer customers would arrive. Every stool would be filled and every booth—primarily with loggers, road crews, or the Forest Service "boys". Truman would shoo any minors out of the main floor of the lodge when beer was being served.

If I was sent away, I'd walk down to the boathouse as dusk set in. The warm evening wind whispered in my face. I could see the shooting-star wildflowers growing between the lowbush huckleberry and splashes of color from the yellow monkeyflowers blooming on the banks of the Toutle.

A fisherman quite often would be whipping his line for a
first cast upstream as he stood on top of Coe's Dam. An otter
would come up from some pocket on the side of the river,
see the fisherman and dive, splashing the water with his
thick tail. As the sun dropped behind the hills, Spirit Lake
assumed an air of mystery and snow-capped Mount St.
Helens showed a different mood just before it was swal-
lowed up by a purple darkness. The distant snowfields were
incandescent and dimly reflected a pinkish glow. Then the
moon rose and the mountain looked as if it belonged in
another world.

When I walked back up to the lodge, I would suddenly
realize how tired I was. It took a real effort as I slowly
climbed the two flights of stairs to my special room high up
in the crow's nest. But I always fell asleep feeling warm and
at peace.

2:

Tumbling Memories

TRUMAN and Auntie Eddie met through my mother, Esther Lapham, in the summer of 1944. My father had deserted the family, and my mom was raising three girls on her own. She had not had a vacation since before the United States entered the war in 1941.

A friend had told her about Mount St. Helens and Spirit Lake, and the serenity and peace sounded wonderful. But she didn't want to go alone. Her sister Eddie, after consulting with her husband, said she'd go, and the two boarded a bus in Seattle and headed for a two-week vacation in southwestern Washington.

Gas rationing forced many people to travel by bus during those days, and Truman often picked up his guests at Castle Rock and drove them in his station wagon the 46 miles east to Spirit Lake. For years we would listen to him retell the story of that first meeting. "I'll be goddamn go to hell if I didn't have to pinch myself to see if I was dreamin' when I saw those two beautiful girls get off the bus," he'd say. "Thought for a minute I'd died and gone to heaven. They sure as hell weren't two old-maid schoolteachers. My daughter, Betty, bet me they would be." They were indeed quite a pair. Mom was a small perky redhead and Auntie Eddie was often told she resembled Katharine

Hepburn because of her dark hair and regal stature.

They returned home to Seattle talking about the beauty of Mount St. Helens and Spirit Lake and about a character there named Harry Truman. It was July, 1944, and Truman had joked about the fact that a man with his same name was running with President Roosevelt and might become vice-president. "We might even be shirt-tail relatives," Truman had boasted.

I can still remember that day in the winter of 1944 when Truman came "a-courtin'" my mom. His shiny maroon Pontiac pulled up in front of our house in Seattle as my two sisters and I peeked through the curtains of the front window. He got out of the car, smoothed his sandy brown hair with his large hand and came up the walk. As Mom opened the door, I thought, "He's a nice-looking man." I also thought he looked particularly clean, like he'd been scrubbed with a brush.

Truman had a big sack of chocolates in his hands and stood there rather awkwardly as he peered down at the three girls—Dayle, 12; Elaine, 7; and me, 11. I don't think Mom had forewarned him about us—his slightly jutting chin dropped down to his chest as we were introduced. I don't know if he had brought the chocolates for us, but he handed the sack to Dayle and helped Mom on with her coat. We dug into the candy. I remember Mom talking later about having a good time with him because he was "a lot of fun and a character." Dayle can remember other times when Truman would arrive and want to freshen up before a date. She was fascinated by the silky pale blue undershirts he wore instead of the T-shirts we'd seen other men wear. But at age 48, Truman's interest in a woman with three kids soon faded.

In 1945, Auntie Eddie and Uncle George separated and eventually divorced. In the spring of 1946, Auntie Eddie decided to take another vacation to Mount St. Helens and Spirit Lake. Since she had no children or responsibilities in Seattle, that seemed a good place to re-examine her life. But after she arrived, Truman told her he needed help with his resort that summer and asked if she would like a job. Auntie Eddie was buoyed by the beautiful, simple life in the wilderness and decided to quit her job at Frederick & Nelson department store in Seattle and move to Spirit Lake.

The next thing we knew, Auntie Eddie had fallen in love with Truman and in November they told us they were married. When I heard the news, the only thing I thought was, "Oh, the man with all the chocolates, the man who looked so clean." Mom, Auntie Eddie and Truman always had a special bond because of how they first met. Truman was always joshing Mom, telling people he "just couldn't figure out which of these two big-city girls I wanted to court. They were both such a couple a dolls." Then he would put his arm around Mom's shoulder and Auntie Eddie would laugh and say, "But Esther couldn't put up with the fact that you never shut your mouth from the time you picked us up at the bus until we reached Spirit Lake." Then he'd go over, buss Auntie Eddie on the cheek, pat her on the bottom and say, "Oh, Edna, I was just flustrated."

When I wrote letters to them I would write, "Dear Auntie Eddie and Uncle Harry." But eventually I just called him Truman like Auntie Eddie did. He seemed to think that was fine.

Auntie Eddie had five nieces, so there was a long string of girls to work summers at Spirit Lake. My older sister Dayle was the first, in the summer of 1947. Dayle was a confident 15-year-old and if Truman gave her any guff, she just tossed it back at him. I'm not sure he liked that because it seemed to irritate him, or perhaps that was just part of his act, too. He called Dayle, "Hot Pants." All the men who came in the lodge for pop or coffee would stumble over their own feet when they saw Dayle, who was pretty and buxom. Auntie Eddie would laugh and say, "If she gets any top-heavier, she'll fall flat on her face." Truman was always very protective of his nieces and never let any of us date the Forest Service boys, the boat boys, or anyone else when we worked there. Nor did he like us talking to them very long.

At the end of the first summer Dayle worked there, I went up to Spirit Lake to learn the routine. Weekends were busy and there was usually a party going on. Since we weren't allowed in the main room of the lodge when there was drinking, Dayle and I would sneak upstairs to the second-floor dormer room. There were two heat registers with big open grates which allowed us to look directly down at the main hall of the lodge. Dayle and I would each lie on our stomachs on the prickly carpet pad—Truman's version of carpeting on the second floor—and watch all the activity below. We could see Auntie Eddie and Truman dancing cheek-to-cheek, each with one arm extended straight out in front, hands clasped, as they took long sliding dance steps. Glasses and beer bottles would be clanking, the cash register would be ringing, the jukebox would be playing and individual conversations would be almost indistinguishable. But above all the noise, we could always hear Truman's cackling laugh and prattle.

He enjoyed discussing politics. If he was upset about anything that involved any governmental agency or taxes, he would snort, "It must have been those sons-a-bitchin' Republicans." He blamed the Republicans for almost everything that didn't go right around Spirit Lake, or anyplace else for that matter. He liked to debate issues, although it was generally a one-sided debate once he got involved. Truman loved any excuse to launch into his red-white-and-blue, star-studded oratory on the skullduggery of politics. He saw himself as the common citizen who could make the most of his right to be critical of the government. He also appreciated the right to vote and missed very few elections.

As Dayle and I lay on the floor looking down, we could hear him greet people, calling someone an "old bastard." That's how we could tell if he was greeting someone he knew and liked; friends were always old bastards. When someone told him something he didn't know, his surprised voice would echo up through the register, "Well I'll be god-damn go to hell."

Almost everybody who stayed at the resort, or visited, knew to keep a flashlight close at hand. For unless Truman was in a partying mood, it was lights out at 10:00 P.M. Sometimes at parties he'd say, "Okay folks, drink up; it's Truman's bewitchin' hour. Lights out in 10 minutes; I'm lockin' this son-of-a-bitchin' place up." He was usually abrupt, as if it had suddenly dawned on him that the next day was going to be busy and he had to be up at 6:00 A.M.

After I had worked there a couple summers, the days of the week seemed to follow a similar pattern. Sundays were busy, particularly for the boat business if it was a nice day. Truman and Red would no sooner gas up the Chris Craft to take a load of people on a one-dollar cruise around the lake than there would be another group wanting to go.

Truman would pilot the speedboat along the 12 miles of shoreline, pointing out the campground and then steering up to the east end of the lake to Harmony Falls. A rustic lodge nestled on the shore of the hillside, with cabins snuggled in the trees above. Truman didn't talk much about his competition at Harmony Falls Lodge and he didn't seem particularly thrilled about the Scout and YMCA camps in the area either, but always pointed them out to his passengers. Truman would stop the boat, take a deep breath and instruct his passengers to do the same, saying, "You'll never smell that fresh clean mountain air back in the city, folks." Truman always stopped at a good vantage point for his passengers to take photos. The rays of the sun glistened behind him on the snow at the top of Mount St. Helens, as the water quietly slapped at the sides of the boat. The beauty of the towering mountain and clear lake enveloped everyone in the boat, but the serene calm was invariably interrupted by Truman, who seldom liked to pause for long.

The ride back was frequently choppy as the wind ruffled the dark green water in the opposite direction. The passengers would sigh as they disembarked and tell Truman what a wonderful ride it was. "Those boats are our meat and potatoes," he liked to say. At the end of a day he'd pull a wad of money out of his pocket to give Auntie Eddie. Some

Sundays he'd take in about $1,500 just on the boats. But if anyone asked about business, he'd either avoid the subject or say, "God, it's tighter than a bull's ass at fly time." He never wanted anyone to know how much money he was making.

Sunday afternoons were always busy for Auntie Eddie, because almost everyone checked out of the cabins and rooms and she did all the bookkeeping. Mondays were awful because every cabin and room had to be cleaned. Sometimes I was so tired by the end of the day that I'd toss and turn all night. Sometimes I would wake with aching joints and get up on my knees on the bed so I could look out my little window where I'd see beams of light sparkling through the tall trees and the glass-smooth surface of Spirit Lake. I felt aglow with the beauty—and besides, Monday was over!

On Tuesday mornings Truman went to town with the laundry, so we had to get up early to count it. Late Tuesday afternoon when he came back, we stored the laundry away in the big cupboards and the walk-in closet. I remember thinking how fresh and clean the laundry all smelled. We would roll up the cotton twine, which held the blue paper around the linen, and in the winter Auntie Eddie would crochet dishcloths and pillow shams from it.

Truman also went shopping on Tuesdays. He would buy fishing gear, which we resold at the lodge. He had poles, nets, flies, spoons, fish eggs, and night crawlers, which he stored in large coffee cans filled with dirt and moss. All the gear was stored in a large glass cabinet at the end of the long bar in the main room of the lodge, and I usually spent Tuesday afternoon restocking it.

Wednesdays we'd wash our own clothes out back in a galvanized tub, scrubbing them on the washboard, and hanging them to dry. Midweek was nice because there wasn't as much to do. Truman had a lawn swing out back, and sometimes we'd all just sit around in the afternoon enjoying the peace and quiet. Frequently Truman's four horses were grazing nearby, and he would brush their coats and they would nibble at his shirt pockets, looking for the sugar cubes he had put there for them. Thursdays were never particularly busy either, so Auntie Eddie and I would go hiking or canoeing. Or Truman would take us for a boat ride up to Harmony Falls.

Early one Thursday morning, Auntie Eddie and I packed a lunch and decided to hike the six and a half miles to Mount Margaret. Truman thought it was a great idea and drove us up past the campground to Duck Bay where the trail began. It hugged one side of the lake. On the other side, there was a hillside with tall stands of fir trees. The lake was a crystal green, and we could see trout darting about in the deep water.

We approached the 150-foot cliff where Harmony Falls spilled its curtain of water. We had to cross Harmony Falls because it was in the trail's path. There was a narrow ledge about halfway up the falls and only one of us could cross at a time. As water cascaded down the giant slabs of basalt, it splashed us and then tumbled down into Spirit Lake. We made our way down the trail next to the waterfall. The quiet solitude was interrupted by the whirring of the generator which provided electricity for Harmony Falls Lodge and its cabins. Auntie Eddie and I went into the rustic old lodge and had a cup of coffee and a piece of huckleberry pie. She laughed and said, "Now don't you tell Truman we gave his competition some business."

Returning to the trail, we passed a couple of dilapidated cabins. Then the route wound through more forest and the hike became more strenuous as the trail went from a carpet of needles to a washboard of pumice rock, left over from an eruption of Mount St. Helens nearly 100 years before. Soon we came to alpine meadows, and streams trickled tiny threads of bright clear water. As we climbed toward Swede Mine, we passed subalpine fir and pine, some gnarled and twisted from late, lingering snows. We walked by clusters of rosy spirea, and then into a vivid meadow of Indian paintbrush. Auntie Eddie explained that thousands of dollars had been spent establishing Swede Mine, but it had only produced three cars of low-grade copper, and the mine was closed in 1929. We sat in lush vegetation that had taken over the area and ate ham-and-cheese sandwiches, surrounded by great gray mountains. A Roosevelt elk, with a large rack of furry horns, stopped and stared at us from behind a snag, then headed for a rock-crested ridge.

On our way back, Auntie Eddie stopped to marvel at the flowers in bloom and put slips in a sack with the hope she could get them to start around the lodge. We could see the boat dock in the distance as the sun slipped behind the hills. Dusk closed in fast, and the stars came out one by one. Everything in front of me seemed blurry and out of focus when we finally trudged home along the cabin lane. Truman came to us with his familiar half-running, arms-swinging walk and a look of consternation on his face. He'd been worried about us, and I think he was getting ready to scold us, like a parent will a lost child. But when he saw how bedraggled we were, his frown turned to a smile and he threw his head back in loud laughter. Truman put his arm around Auntie Eddie as we walked back to the lodge together.

Fridays we began preparations for the onslaught of the busy weekend and Truman would go shopping in Longview or Centralia. He usually took Boy with him. Boy sat inside the pickup next to Truman and looked out the window, just like another person. On the doors of the pickup, it said, "Mt. St. Helens Lodge, Spirit Lake, Harry Truman."

Truman would return home with a side of pork; several beef roasts; a case of eggs; a couple cases of bread; pounds of butter, hot dogs and hamburger; plus three of his favorite foods—chicken liver, cow brains, and buttermilk. Sometimes he brought back ice cream which had been packed in dry ice.

Routinely, Auntie Eddie would ask, "Didn't you buy the kids some milk?" Truman would say, "What in the hell for? They've got all the goddamn pop they can drink right down in the basement." She usually got mad at him for not getting something on the shopping list—always something he didn't particularly like. They had weekly disagreements about hamburger buns. She always put them on the grocery list and Truman always returned without them, saying he forgot.

I loved the warm sunny days. Gilbert, the cat, would lie on the dock and peer over the edge watching the fish play hide-and-go-seek between the snags in the water. Gilbert's head swayed back and forth, and then he'd begin stalking the fish as he walked on the dock. Before long, he'd jump in after them, then swim to shore while we laughed. Gilbert was the only cat I ever saw swim. "Look at that damn Gilbert," Truman would say. "No one'd believe it if they didn't see it for themselves." He'd say the same thing when Gilbert would accompany Boy around the parking lot and follow Boy's example, lifting his leg and leaving a little trademark on car tires.

Sometimes we'd toss chunks of volcanic pumice in the lake to see how long they would float. The lake was so clear we could still see the holes in the pumice as it sunk 30 feet and came to rest on the bottom amid the decayed logs and tree stumps. When people commented on this unusual phenomenon, Truman would say, "Yes, this is the place where the goddamn logs sink and the rocks float."

Across the headwaters of the Toutle River, there were two cabins which Truman only rented when all the others were full. One was Truman's original home, which he called Honeymoon Cabin. I liked to clean Honeymoon Cabin because it was over along a quiet tree-lined trail at the lake's edge. The cabin was more like an old house which had been abandoned, with a big front porch where I'd sit and look out at the lake or up at the mountain. There I could see a large section of Truman's sprawling 50-acre resort with 15 or 20 cabins scattered between the tall conifers.

Back along the trail, my footsteps always sounded hollow when I walked on the dense carpet of fir needles and humus

from decayed trees hundreds of years old. I'd look at the
beautiful maidenhair ferns, the delicate yellow violets or
dainty calypso orchids, with their flowers balancing precariously at the top of four-inch stems. I would see bear and
cougar droppings along the trail and I often watched deer
or elk as they gracefully sailed into underbrush up the steep
hillside next to the trail.

Mount St. Helens and Spirit Lake were a photographer's
joy. The snow-capped peak of the mountain always domi-
nated the scene, and early in the morning it was easy to take
superb pictures of the mirror image of the mountain reflected on Spirit Lake. Everyone who ever worked at Spirit
Lake ended up in some professional photographer's picture. Auntie Ruth, Eddie's younger sister, was a beauty
queen in Seattle and was a particular favorite of the photographers. Truman frequently was in pictures, too, but only at
a distance so he couldn't be recognized. Usually he was
pictured with his yachting cap perched on the back of his
head, standing in one of his speedboats.

Those days, Truman didn't like it when reporters came
around, and he never gave interviews. But he'd always tell
photographers where he thought the best vantage points
were. And he also gave them free advice on how to take their
pictures. "Now you boys, you've gotta put a human being in
the goddamn thing. The public's not just interested in that
goddamn ol' mountain and lake," he'd say. "Now you get a
nice little speedboat in the foreground, or a man fishing and
you put the human element in the thing, because a little
human interest is what means so much to the goddamn
public."

During the summer months wildflowers would follow the
melting snow in the mountain meadows with a profusion of
bright blossoms. The area around the lodge was always alive
with the color of flowers, too. Auntie Eddie really loved
flowers and she and Truman enjoyed their roles as amateur
botanists, sharing their knowledge of plants with their
guests. Truman had given her a handsome book on moun-

tain wildflowers of the Pacific Northwest as a birthday present one year and that book was usually close at hand. Late in the winter, when there was still snow on the ground, Auntie Eddie would start seeds and bulbs in boxes at the orchard 15 miles down the highway. When spring came, she would transfer them to the ground around the lodge and she would transplant flaming orange and red Indian paintbrush from the high meadows to the flower beds around the sign at the entrance to Truman's resort. She planted begonias behind the lodge near the base of the giant fir tree by the lawn swing. Truman made planter boxes for the front porch and Auntie Eddie filled them with her flowers. The front porch was 25 feet long and 15 feet deep and we'd often sit there by the signs that said, "No Minors" and "Boats— Motors—Cabins." Truman couldn't sit still longer than two minutes, of course, so he'd get up and walk over to one of Auntie Eddie's hanging baskets where he'd cup a fragile fuchsia blossom in his rough hand and say, "Now, look at that. Isn't that the most beautiful thing you ever saw? Eddie can make any goddamn thing grow."

3:

Early Times

Harry Truman was born in West Virginia in October of 1896. His parents were Newberry and Rosa Belle Truman and he was their first child, born in a log cabin in the tiny community of Ivydale, northeast of Charleston, where even today only 200 people live. They called the boy Harry R. Truman, although later no one would know what the R stood for and even Truman himself wasn't sure what day in October he had been born on. He settled on October 30 and celebrated his birthday then.

Most of West Virginia was forest land—rolling green hills and wooded valleys of white oak and sycamore—and it was only natural for generations of Trumans to be woodsmen and loggers. But by the time young Harry turned 11, much of the Appalachian Mountains had been logged off and families like the Trumans were being lured west. They heard tales about Washington, which had only been a state for 17 years, and how it had beauty, cheap land, and a burgeoning timber industry. It was decided that much of the Truman clan would head west; Grandfather Elijah, his three grown sons, Floyd, Marion and Newberry—Harry's father—and all their families. By now, Harry had a three-year-old sister, Geraldine. The year was 1907, and Theodore Roosevelt was President.

28

Harry Truman was always proud of his West Virginia heritage and on cold winter nights in his lodge at Spirit Lake he often reminisced about how the Trumans traveled west by train, bringing enough food for the nine-day trip— cornbread and home-cured ham, apples and home-canned beans. The men carried rifles and jugs of corn whiskey.

"There we were, out in the middle of the goddamn plains," Truman remembered. "We'd already crossed the Mississippi. That country was flatter than pee on a plate and West Virginians don't like flat country. At some of the stations, we saw Indians, all dressed up in their fancy garb.

"The train stopped at some no-name place to put on water and we took the coon dogs out for a pee. I tied my hounds up for a few minutes, figuring my uncles would get them when they got their own dogs, and I went back on board for some supper. Well about 10 miles out, I started lookin' for my goddamn dogs. I couldn't find them and I raised hell. Then I pulled the emergency cord and stopped the whole goddamn train; everything went flyin' and scared the livin' hell out of everyone, but I knew my hounds couldn't survive in that God-forsaken place. I told them they better back up that goddamn train so as I could get my goddamn dogs, or I'd jump off the train. I would have, too. But they backed the train up, and I'll tell you, those damn dogs were happier than hell to see me."

Eight days out of West Virginia the train reached the Columbia River. The food had gone stale, and the railroad coach smelled of sweat, spilled whiskey, and dogs. There were no bridges, and the train was ferried across the mighty river on barges near Portland.

Like many families who came west, the Trumans first settled in the lowlands where the men tried to earn enough money to buy a farm. They started out in Napavine, in southwest Washington State. Napavine was a bustling community in those days, a major train depot where farmers brought their produce, cattle and hogs to be marketed in nearby Chehalis and Centralia. It was surrounded by rolling green hills and seemed a fine place to live for a while.

Newberry Truman and his brothers bought a donkey engine in Napavine. It was a strange-looking logging contraption with double drums and cables to pull logs out of the woods, doing the work of many oxen. The Trumans had one of the first donkey engines in the area.

Before long, the Trumans moved to the backwoods of eastern Lewis County, for they were mountain people who depended on the forests for survival. That wilderness was reminiscent of their land in West Virginia, although there was no comparing the soil and climate. The soil in West Virginia was rocky and they sometimes had to carry dirt to cover their corn. In Washington there was deep sandy soil, which could be cultivated and where farms would prosper.

It took two days and nights for the Trumans to make the 45-mile trip in their wagons to their new 160-acre farm. The road was a combination of mudholes and plank, and was called a corduroy or puncheon road. Truman remembered it later as "the bumpiest thing I ever rode on." It was too expensive to blast stumps in those days, so the roads— narrow, crooked, muddy and overhung with dense timber —just wound around them. Each traveler carried an ax, and when two wagons met, the drivers went to work and chopped out a turn-out. The Trumans drove their wagons high up into the hills past unpainted shacks and clapboard houses where families of loggers lived, east through Mossy-rock and Riffe, and finally to Nesika.

Nesika was only two or three houses then; later a post office was added. In the narrow valley, farms alternated with patches of timber. It was in this valley alongside the Cowlitz River that Newberry Truman worked as a hunter, farmer and logger. Their nearest neighbor was the family of Floyd Riffe, who had founded the Baptist church in the tiny town of Osborne in 1900, and served as the town's doctor, free of charge. Grateful citizens changed the town's name to Riffe. But several years later the Riffes moved six miles east to Nesika, and when Newberry Truman carved out his homestead, it bordered the Riffe farm. Young Harry became good friends with the Riffes' son Jesse, and together they went to school in Glenoma, seven miles away.

Harry would become skilled at fishing, hunting and trapping. Regulations were slowly being established in the area, but folks from the hills of West Virginia weren't accustomed to laws governing fishing, hunting and trapping — or distilling. Harry learned that, too.

Neighbors meant a lot to each other in those days. It was a community effort to clear land or raise a house. People didn't usually work for cash, but exchanged good deeds or received supplies for their work. The Trumans' house was constructed of hand-split cedar boards, as were the barn and the outbuildings. The wood came from the Trumans' land, where they felled large trees, sometimes eight or nine feet in diameter. Then they cut them into six-foot lengths by hand, using an eleven-foot cross-cut saw. Some logs were cut into shingle-bolt lengths, usually sixteen inches. These were split into shakes and shingles with a froe, a knifelike tool that was laid on a shingle bolt. A smart blow from a mallet would cause the froe to split off a perfect sixteen-inch shingle. Years later Harry Truman would use the knowledge he had gained as a boy to build his lodge, cabins, restaurant, and boathouse. All the shakes covering his buildings at the resort were hand-split by him and his carpenter friends. Truman could split as many as 1,000 shakes in a day.

The Trumans were primarily loggers, but they also did some farming — raising dairy cows and hogs. Families in the area had periodic hog drives to Chehalis. Other times, they slaughtered hogs on the farm and smoked ham and slabs of bacon for weeks over fires of green vine maple. They made their own soap and candles from tallow, dried their own vegetables and fruit, and drew water from a well with a wooden bucket. Kerosene lamps were used for light.

Harry Truman often rode a horse to school with his friends Jesse Riffe and Earl Coleman. Charlie Osborne, now 84, was another of Harry's good friends and school chums. Charlie and Harry only lived a mile apart and they often spent many evenings riding their bicycles together at Harry's house. Once they rode their bicycles 45 miles to Chehalis to see a circus. "We left about 4:00 A.M.," Charlie recalls, "Harry, Ezra Blankenship, and I. In those days we only had one-speed bicycles and we'd push them up one hill and coast them down another. There wasn't much road at all. It was 45 miles of plank and corduroy, and we just went bumpety, bumpety, bump all the way to the road to Chehalis. We left our bicycles in the livery stable, and we took off our overalls, which we had on over our Sunday go-to-meetin' britches. We always got dressed up when we went to town."

The three boys rode an electric streetcar, which ran between Chehalis and Centralia, and went to watch the circus. "They were real circuses in those days," Charlie remembers. "The parade was better than the whole circus is today; it would be two or three miles long. There were all kinds of animals in their cages, and clowns and the calliope. Frankly, I'm not sure what the circus itself was like, because I was so tired after riding my bicycle 45 miles that I just nodded off and slept through most of it. Harry and Ezra went right back home that night, but my legs were so knotted up with charley horses, that I got a room in a hotel and stayed in Chehalis. I was 15 at the time."

Charlie and Jesse Riffe still have strong memories of the members of the Truman family. They remember Newberry as an active, wiry man, whom Harry came to resemble closely. Both also shared a certain daredevil spirit. Charlie and Jesse remember Harry's mother Rosa as a woman quite similar to Newberry and Harry—fast-talking, loud, and outspoken, Jesse recalls, "not the soft, tender, friendly sort of mother." They also remember her strong Baptist faith. Neither Harry nor his sister Geraldine would become Baptists, but Rosa did have one Baptist ally in the house, Shirley Ice, an orphaned nephew she took into the Truman home as a member of the family. Ironically, Ice's son Richard was to become a Baptist minister who would one day preside over the memorial service for Harry Truman.

Jesse and Charlie remember Harry as being full of curiosity and mischief in his school days. "If Harry wasn't getting into mischief, he was getting in the way," Charlie says. "Harry and I used to get in the Cowlitz River with an outboard motor and he'd hit the high rough parts of the water and it didn't bother him a bit. He was devilish. The rougher it was, the better he liked it and if he got dumped out he'd get to shore some way, even though he couldn't swim a lick."

A couple times a year the Trumans and the Osbornes would travel together to Chehalis for supplies. The journey would take two days and nights in their horse-pulled wagons. "We'd get down to Salkum and we'd feed our horses," Charlie recalls. "We had a 'grub box' for food and we'd brew our own coffee on a campfire and eat, then we'd get into town maybe late that night. We'd have our eats and put the horses up in the livery stable and stay overnight and the next morning we'd go out and buy groceries and things we had to have. Usually there was someone who got sidetracked in the saloon. My dad needed to buy flour by the ton because he raised 10 children. All they did in those days was work and raise kids."

In the early 1900s, the members of Mossyrock Grange decided they needed a new high school. It was completed in 1910 and is still standing—a four-room building with a wood furnace. There were four teachers when it opened, and the superintendent taught a class or two. The enrollment of the Mossyrock High School was 75 students. It was thirteen miles from the Truman farm, and four from Charlie Osborne's. Since Harry's family had horses, he frequently rode one to school and met Charlie on the way. Sometimes they rode their bicycles.

Ted and Emma Landes, who still live near Mossyrock, in Cinebar, were schoolmates of Harry, although they were not

members of his 1917 graduating class, which was the first
class to graduate with more than one student. Ted Landes
remembers the time when the principal called Harry and
the other boys into a room where strange bowls sat on the
floor. "Now these are toilets, boys," the principal said, "and
when you flush them they make quite a bit of noise, so I
don't want any of you jumping out the window or out into
the hall."

All of Harry Truman's school chums remember that he
had several hunting dogs and that once he was the center of
attention because he killed a bear—quite a feat for a young
man of 15.

Baseball was a particularly popular sport in the early
days, but roads were poor and high schools too far apart for
competition between schools. So the high school boys
played against adults in the community, and that was how
Harry met his good friend Lawrence Rakes, a school-
teacher who would enlist with Harry during World War I.
Harry's friends remember him as being a very bright young
man. Harry's grade average after four years of high school
was 86.8 out of 100. He took courses in English, algebra,
geometry, math, and bookkeeping, as well as botany,
physics, physiology, and several history classes. But Grace
Sears Finstad, a classmate of Harry, remembers him as a
"stinker." "He was smart all right," she recalls. "He thought
he was the 'cock of the walk.' He was good-looking and all
the girls liked him. You couldn't help but like him; he'd talk
to anyone and he was always neat and clean. But he was a
cocky guy." He was also someone who always seemed to use
swear words, even as a youth. Says Charlie Osborne: "Harry
just couldn't talk without cussin'."

Harry quit school for a year. It wasn't unusual then for
students to take longer than four years to graduate from
high school. There was work to be done and the boys
wanted to earn money. He worked at the Glenoma School,
east of Nesika and Riffe, and got odd jobs through friends.
He also worked for the McDonell family, who lived across

from the school. Harry lived with the McDonells for almost
a year.

Andrew McDonell, a baseball buddy of Harry, had two
beautiful sisters—Mary and Bernadette, who is still known
as Dude. Today she is a bright and delightful 84-year-old
woman. Dude McDonell also remembers Harry's popularity
with the girls in school. "Hazel Crawford was sweet on
Harry," she recalls. "One day my girlfriend and I went to get
Hazel's brother with a team of horses and a wagon full of
hay. But we wanted Harry to ourselves, so we hid him under
the hay. He was a good sport; he didn't make a peep when
we picked up Hazel's brother, not even when Hazel came
out and asked about him."

Dude McDonell's mother was the backbone of the family
and decided to take in boarders to help make ends meet.
She charged $22 a month for room and board, and the
farmhouse got so crowded with four children and five
boarders that an extra house was built for the women to
stay in. Four of the boarders were teachers; the other was
Harry. Dude remembers taking pictures and always trying
to get people to pose in unusual circumstances. Once,
she talked Harry into dressing up like a girl and took his
picture—a picture she still keeps.

Winter was a grand time up in eastern Lewis County.
Dude remembers Harry building homemade skis, and riding horses with Harry in the light snow. And she remembers
dances at Glenoma School when the kids from Mossyrock
came and they danced until her mother fixed a midnight
supper for everyone. "We lived in a valley with a big hill
,behind the ranch," she says. "Harry and I used to climb to
the top of the hill and you could see Mount Rainier, Mount
St. Helens and all over. He was a lot of fun."

Truman returned to Mossyrock High School as a senior.
Charlie Osborne remembers Truman's return vividly because that was when Harry bought his first car and the two
rode to school in style. The car was a Metz roadster with
friction drive. Jesse Riffe remembers the Metz well: "Harry

would fix up that car and get it running good and then he'd take it out on the highway, run it as fast as he could, wreck it, bring it back, fix it up, and do it all over again. I remember one time he even rolled it over, but he never hurt anybody and he never hurt himself." That was the beginning of Harry's lifelong love affair with the automobile. Harry was the only high school student to own his own car and, indeed, one of the few people in Riffe or Nesika who owned one.

There were five boys and two girls who graduated from the first Mossyrock Viking class of 1917 and their picture still hangs in the Mossyrock High School lunchroom. They were Harry Truman, Jesse Riffe, Ernest Gowen, Charlie Osborne, Fred Martin, Ella Jordan, and Laura Fraser.

The first home of Harry Truman and the homes and farms of many early settlers of Nesika and Riffe were later covered by the 23-mile-long reservoir created by the massive Mossyrock Dam on the Cowlitz River. Before the dam was finished in 1969, 213 graves were moved from the Riffe and Smith cemeteries. The land where Harry Truman grew up riding his bicycle, playing baseball, and chasing pretty girls is gone forever.

4: War and Prohibition

THE military postcard with the fading blue ink was addressed to Mr. Jesse Riffe, Nesika, Washington, U.S.A. The return address read, "Harry Truman, 100 Aero Sq'dn., American Expeditionary Force, France." On the front was the purple stamp of the military censor and his signature: 1st Lt. F. U. Platt. Truman's message read:

Still Kicking   Somewhere in France
                                              Sept. – 3 – 1918 –
   Dear Jess—It has been a long time since I heard from you. The weather is fine here now and we are giving the Germans h——. Our boys are whipping them in every mode or way of fighting—Write me a long letter. Hello to Charlie—Best wishes to all—Harry

Truman had enlisted with the two Rakes brothers and classmate Fred Martin in Centralia in July of 1917. Like many young men his age, he had enlisted out of patriotism fueled by splendid dreams of flying missions in the skies over France. But he was trained as an aeromechanic and electrician and was assigned to the 7th Squad of the 100th Aero Squadron. Then came the trip across the country— his first long train ride since he had traveled from West

Virginia to Washington at age 11. By October, Truman had
joined his comrades in arms of the Aero Squadron, which
was a bombardment squadron stationed at Hazelhurst
Field, New York. Under a veil of secrecy, the squadron was
shipped to Halifax, Nova Scotia, one of four Canadian ports
used by ships carrying troops overseas during World War I.

At Halifax, Truman boarded the *Tuscania,* a 14,400-ton
British steamship of the Anchor Line, which was serving as
a transport for American troops. The troopships traveled
in convoys which were assigned to clear the sea lanes of
German submarines. The winter of 1917-1918 was one of
the bitterest in memory and the stormy North Atlantic
became as much an enemy as the German submarines.
During the 14-day crossing, Truman could sleep only by
bracing himself in his bunk. His arms and legs ached from
hanging onto lines and ladders. "I was so goddamn seasick,"
he said later, "that I didn't care if the son-of-a-bitchin' tub
rolled clean over."

The *Tuscania*'s torturous crossing was almost over on
February 5, 1918; the troopship was only 10 miles from the
Irish coastline, which could be just faintly seen off the starboard side. Truman was among the troops watching boxing
matches when a German torpedo slammed into the ship's
boiler room. "It scared the living hell out of me," Truman
later recalled. "Everything went black."

The ship listed badly and flares were lighted on every
deck to replace the *Tuscania*'s failed lighting system, destroyed by the initial explosion. Confusion was everywhere.
Men struggled into lifeboats, but the starboard list lifted the
lifeboats on the port side so high they were useless. While
some men jumped, others fell overboard in the chill darkness before the ship sank. The survivors were taken to the
ports of Buncrana and Larne in northern Ireland and to
Islay in southern Scotland. Newspapers in the United States
were filled for days with accounts of the sinking, and up-
dated daily lists of survivors—lists which did not initially
include Truman's name, causing his parents great concern.

After five long days, Truman's name finally appeared—
he'd been rescued. The final accounting of troops in the
sinking of the *Tuscania* was 2,235 saved and 166 lost.

Truman described the sinking and his rescue in a letter
sent to his mother from England on Valentine's Day.

I don't know what the United States papers said
about the wreck of the *Tuscania,* but feel sure they gave
an account of it but not in a way I can relate it when I
come home....The lifeboat I was in smashed up but I
made it to a sub destroyer all right and only got wet.

We lost everything we had, coats, hats and everything
that was loose. I happened to have my pictures in my
pocket and saved them.... I suppose the sinking of the
boat caused much excitement over there because it was
the first American transport to be torpedoed, but there
wasn't many lost, only five of my friends from our
squadron. Tell Dad that I am getting along fine and
send love to the kids, and don't worry about me for I will
get back all right. With love, from Harry.

While he was in England, Truman also wrote to Dude
McDonell. He enclosed a picture of himself and a friend.
Both were in full uniform, except for Truman's hat. He
explained to Dude that he had lost his uniform hat when
the *Tuscania* was sunk and that someone in Ireland had
given him the civilian hat he was wearing.

Truman's time in England was largely uneventful. He
worked as an airplane mechanic and electrician and wrote
home that he was "having a fine time such as it is, for there
is not very much variety here." The work did allow him
plenty of spare time to travel and he covered most of
England and Ireland, although the 22-year-old mechanic
from Nesika, Washington, found the countries "cannot
compare with the old U.S.A. at all."

Then Truman was transferred to France and worked day
and night keeping planes in shape for combat patrols. He
also may have become a combat pilot himself, as many of the

best young mechanics did. At any rate, years later in his lodge at Spirit Lake, he would tell people he had. He would tell of flying in the open cockpits of the French-made Spad biplanes, a leather cap on his head, a white silk scarf around his neck "flapping in the breeze." Like many war stories, they were tales that improved with each telling, and they fit Truman's lifelong image of himself as a daredevil— whether they were all true or not. There is no question, though, that Truman did fly planes in later years—a skill he may well have learned during the war in France.

Early in 1918, Truman wrote his mother from England saying, "I wish I was back home again." In late October, 1918, Truman's 100th Aero Squadron was assigned to the newly formed Second Army's 2nd Day Bombardment Group, which flew DeHavillands. On November 11, 1918, members of the newly formed group were preparing to take off from Ourches Airfield along the Meuse River on their first bombing mission when they were notified that the armistice had been signed.

In June of 1919, Truman got his wish. He was demobilized at Mitchell Field, New York, and took a troop train across the continent for the last time, as did his buddy Charlie Osborne. The two young veterans were happy to see the rich flatland of the Cowlitz River Valley and even happier to see their homes in the tall timber wilderness of eastern Lewis County.

But the war changed Truman, as it did so many of the young men who served in France. His good friend Charlie Osborne, who saw action in the infantry in some of the war's bitterest battles, returned to Washington State with his ambition gone and his education spoiled. And Osborne found his friend Truman changed, too. "He became kind of a loner, I think. We never discussed the war much after we came home. We wanted to forget it."

Not long after Truman's return home he married Helen Hughes, the daughter of a sawmill owner in the area. On March 11, 1922, they had a daughter and named her Betty.

But there was sadness, too. On May 8, 1923, Truman's father, Newberry, was killed in a logging accident at Lacamas, about 25 miles west of Nesika. The elder Trumans had recently moved to Chehalis and had only lived there eight days when the accident occurred. Newberry had been working with a logging crew when a dangerous maneuver was required with a donkey engine. The other members of the crew refused to participate, but Newberry Truman volunteered and was crushed between two logs.

"He said, 'That's not too dangerous for me,'" Charlie Osborne recalls, "and he went down there and got killed. Harry's dad was a daredevil like Harry; I don't know exactly how the accident happened but logging is a hazardous job. I worked in the woods for six months and gave it up. Logs have no respect for anybody."

Harry Truman was then working as a mechanic for St. John Motors, a Ford dealership in Chehalis, using the skills he learned in the Air Corps. Charlie Osborne was an auto mechanic, too, and worked for the Buick-Dodge garage across the street. To Ed Lowry—who worked beside Truman as a mechanic at the Ford dealer's—Truman was a good mechanic who swore a lot but was always "hospitable and gentlemanly." Truman also kept to himself, seldom confiding in his fellow workers. It wasn't until later that Lowry learned that Truman was married during the time they were working together.

Truman soon tired of the day-to-day humdrum of a mechanic's life. He had heard tales that "you could pick gold off the bushes in Nevada" and he went there hoping to find fortune as a prospector. But Truman found prospecting was hard work—too hard. Bootlegging was easier.

In many ways, it was also a perfect match of man and profession. Truman liked his liquor, and prohibition profoundly offended him. He had fought for his country in France and now that country was telling him he couldn't have a drink. Truman was ambitious and full of initiative; he didn't mind taking risks: he thrived in crisis situations. And fast cars, required equipment for a rumrunner, had always been among his favorite things. Soon Truman was picking up liquor smuggled into San Francisco and running it up to southwestern Washington. Whorehouses on the coast in Aberdeen and Hoquiam were among his regular stops then, as he told friend George Bowers—as was the home of a young lady named Rosalie. He would tell his best male friends about her for years afterward.

But the nature of the bootlegging business started to change from a haven for small independent operators to a big business controlled by gangsters. Truman had worked with a gang in California, but there were the inevitable disagreements over money and territory, and Truman left the state just a few steps ahead of some people who were after him. "I got in trouble with some big guys," Truman told George Bowers. "Things got hotter than hell." Among the possessions that Truman brought back from California was a .45-caliber Thompson submachine gun, popular with gangsters of that era.

Truman sought refuge in Chehalis, and operated a small gas station and repair shop called Harry's Sudden Service. Truman and his wife Helen had a bungalow next door to the station. He continued to sell bootleg whiskey and moonshine on the side, as many small businesses did then. But his refuge was not well-enough hidden—he was not very good at keeping a low profile—and Truman soon heard that the people he had fled from in California were hot on his trail again. So Harry's Sudden Service closed abruptly in 1926 and Truman packed his wife, his daughter, and his submachine gun off to a place where he thought no one could find them—the back country wilderness around Spirit Lake and Mount St. Helens. He began by operating a small gas station and log cabin grocery and renting a few boats, a business he shared with Jack Nelson. But the two partners had words and soon parted ways. Nelson went across Spirit Lake to build and operate his own lodge at Harmony Falls. Truman stayed to operate the business and built a large log

home at the headwaters of the North Fork of the Toutle
River. It was indeed the isolated spot Truman had sought.

"At that time, you had to wait until all the snow and
everything was gone because the roads were so chuckholey
and muddy," recalls friend Wes Lamon. "You only had July
and August that you could possibly get up there; otherwise,
it was all snowed in." The road to Spirit Lake used to follow
the South Fork of the Toutle for a short distance and then
jolted over Green Mountain. "That old puncheon road was
just barely cut out between the big fir trees," says Wes, "and if
you met anybody, you had to back up or cut a road around
them."

The isolation at Spirit Lake hid Truman from his pur-
suers, but it also took its toll on his personal life. First his
daughter, Betty, had to be sent to stay with Jesse and Lucy
Riffe in Nesika; there was no school near Spirit Lake. Later
she was sent to a Catholic boarding school, and for a time
lived with her grandmother Rosa Belle. Finally, Truman's
wife Helen decided that life in the isolated wilderness was
not the one she wanted, so she moved back to the valley.
Their divorce followed.

The place was so isolated that Truman resumed his bootlegging business to make more money. Cy Jacques, who
worked on trails for the Forest Service at that time, remembers frequent visits to Truman's place to buy whiskey.

"We used to go up to Truman's pretty nearly every night
and get a bottle of moonshine from him," Cy, now 74,
recalls. "Sometimes we'd go to Truman's and stay a day. He
charged $1.50 for a short pint; they were flat little whiskey
bottles that held 10 to 12 ounces. Harry made good money
on moonshine at $1.50. My God! We were only making $3
a day!"

Truman's first home at Spirit Lake was in a cabin across
the headwaters of the North Toutle. Near there, Cy remembers, is where Truman hid one of his stills. "Harry had
a still down on Studebaker Creek," he says. "He also had
one across the lake somewhere."

Truman told other friends about his stills. He told Chuck
Tonn of the Forest Service about the still down by
Studebaker Creek and about a still near Hofstad Creek,
adjacent to the orchard. Truman told friend George Bowers
about the still he kept in a cave not far from the boat dock by
the Toutle and he showed George the labels he used to put
on his moonshine—labels that said *Panther Pee.*

That same cave was where Truman kept some of the
game he poached. "Harry shot bear and elk; he was a great
old poacher, Harry was," George recalls. "But he would
never shoot animals just for sport; he'd do it because he
needed some goddamn food, something to eat."

Despite his busy bootlegging and poaching, Truman still
found time to improve his legitimate business at the lodge.
Author Joseph P. Hazard visited Truman's lodge and described the scene in a book called *Snow Sentinels of the Pacific
Northwest,* published in 1932.

"Spirit Lake and Mount St. Helens are now open to the
public all the year around," Hazard wrote. "This winter, the
snow at the lake is nine feet deep. But Mount St. Helens
Lodge is cozy inside, and the outside is another winter
paradise. The snow line is six miles below the lake. The
lodge attendant meets all visitors with skis and snowshoes
and escorts them from the snow line to the lake. This season, the growing popularity of the new winter sports region
demands advance reservations."

5:

Building Years

THE rugged country around Spirit Lake and Mount St. Helens was often harsh and unforgiving, and it exacted a price from those few who chose to live there year-round. Thanksgiving of 1930, a tornado roared through the Spirit Lake area. It snapped trees up to five feet in diameter, carrying them upright for as far as a quarter-mile. Some trees were tossed far out into the lake.

Injuries and deaths were common occurrences in the wilds. They were accepted—it was part of living with nature. In his book *The Story of Lige Coalman,* author Victor H. White recalls the saga of Emil Lange, the owner of a small sawmill at Dry Gulch, two miles from Truman's lodge. In 1933, the burly Lange died of a heart attack while standing in the mud road in front of his home. It was a time of another torrential rainstorm and the Toutle at Dry Gulch had turned into a raging river. But Lange's neighbors thought it was important to carry his body out of the wilderness so he could be buried in a cemetery in the lowlands. Four men—Truman, Spirit Lake ranger Harold Samuelson, and Lige Coalman from the nearby Y.M.C.A. camp and his son, Elrod—carried the corpse across the Toutle, over the hills and down steep trails. "When we returned to Spirit Lake—tired, wet and weary," Coalman wrote in his diary, "we had hiked 40 miles that day, half of it carrying the 250-pound weight of a dead man. But we all felt it was a good service to a fine neighbor and friend."

The people living far from doctors often found seemingly insignificant injuries turned serious. Truman himself suffered a leg injury skiing about that time and it seemed to be healing when blood poisoning developed. The lodge was totally snowed in so Lige Coalman and his son put Truman on a toboggan and pulled him in the deep snow for five hours to the place on the road where three "snow-breaking" Ford roadsters waited. The three cars were tied together and each had chains on all four wheels. They simply rammed their way through the snowdrifts until they reached the open road, where Truman was transferred to a car which took him to Kelso.

The rugged country attracted rugged individuals who enjoyed the solitude of the raw frontier and valued the friendship of the few people they saw frequently. Many of Truman's best friends—and best customers, too—came from the ranks of the men of the U.S. Forest Service, who patrolled the 1.5 million acres of the Columbia National Forest, which included Spirit Lake and Mount St. Helens as well as Mount Adams, Mount Margaret, and the Goat Rocks Wilderness. The Forest Service men helped manage the timber and the wildlife, and they watched over the watersheds and fought fires.

One of Truman's best friends in the Forest Service was Harold Samuelson, who first was assigned to the Spirit Lake area in the early 1920s and stayed until he retired in 1958. He was known as the Ranger of Spirit Lake; everyone fondly called him Sam. He and Truman were not much alike in character or temperament—Sam was a tall, slim man with a quiet manner who didn't drink—but the two shared a strong sense of loyalty and respect. Sam often visited Truman's lodge, but always waited for an invitation before entering the kitchen, where Truman greeted him robustly.

For several years, there was a Forest Service lookout station atop the three-quarter-mile summit of Mount St. Helens. Ken MacDonald worked there the last two summers it was used, living alone in the 12-by-12-foot-square house with the cupola on top, existing on dehydrated food and earning $165 a month, which included a $50 bonus for the isolated assignment. "Being a lookout on the top of Mount St. Helens was like being in an airplane," Ken recalls. "My head was either in the clouds or I was looking down on them." MacDonald was seldom lonely in his summer post. Parties of climbers came to the summit every few days. MacDonald himself climbed the mountain some 40 times and once raced a friend from Spirit Lake to the top in only four hours—two hours less than usual. MacDonald saw no fires in his two summers on the summit, and in 1927 the Forest Service removed the lookout.

Another of Truman's neighbors was Lige Coalman, who joined the staff of the Y.M.C.A. camp at Spirit Lake in 1925 and lived there year-round until 1937. Truman liked Coalman, but he considered the camp's young visitors to be a nuisance when they came exploring, especially since they had little money to spend. He coined colorful terms for them—the kindest of which was "little buggers."

Truman did welcome the expanded development of the Spirit Lake campground in 1938 and 1939—a project of Roosevelt's Civilian Conservation Corps under the supervision of Jim Langdon, another of Truman's good friends in the Forest Service. He saw the improved campground facilities as a boon to his boat business—and it was. But he later changed his mind about the campground and its occupants, who he accused of stealing things from his resort, and he began calling the campers "goddamn squatters."

Truman had no complaints, though, about the cast and crew from the movie *God's Country and the Woman*, which was filmed in the Toutle River valley in 1936. The movie people filled his resort, and years later Truman would tell tales about the friendship he had struck up with Jack Warner, the legendary studio head. Everyone in the area had tales to tell

about the movie; it was the biggest thing to happen there in
years. They talked about stars Beverly Roberts, Alan Hale,
and George Brent—who, the story went, refused to wear
some of the old clothes required in one of the scenes because he considered himself such a dandy. They talked
about how the loggers helped build the massive log jam on
the Toutle in the gorge near Camp Cowlitz—which gave it
the name Hollywood Gorge from then on. And they talked
about the big train-wreck scene and the railroad trestle that
was built for the movie, about seven miles up the Spirit Lake
Highway from Castle Rock.

But what meant far more to Truman was the money
which the movie people spent. He was working hard to
improve and expand his resort and he had had rate
schedules printed up which said:

Cabins for Rent:
2 People: per day, $2.50; per week, $12.50.
4 People: per day, $3.00; per week, $17.50.
Cabins furnished, except bedding.
Electric Lights.

Boats for Rent:
Rowboats: per day, $1.50; per week, $7.00
Outboard Motor Boats: per hour, $1.25; per day, $7.00
Sightseeing Launch: 50 cents per person

Fishermen's Supplies:
Tackle for sale or rent. Licenses here.

LUNCH COUNTER AND STORE
Service Station   Gas and Oil
HARRY TRUMAN, PROPRIETOR
Spirit Lake, Washington
(Elevation of Spirit Lake . . . . 3200 ft.)
(Elevation of Mountain . . . . 9761 ft.)

A year before the movie was filmed, Truman had married for a second time. His pattern of courtship was remarkably similar to one he would follow 10 years later. Truman was dating Frances Powers of Chehalis, but one time when he came to call, Marjorie Bennett Brown was visiting. He soon transferred his amorous attention to her. Marge, a University of Washington graduate, was a French teacher who had recently been divorced. She was five years younger than Truman's 39 years and she already knew him slightly, since she and her former husband had once gone camping with Truman and Helen. Marge was taken by Truman's ruddy radiance and flirtatious spirit, and he didn't seem to mind the fact that she had a nine-year-old daughter, Joan. Marjorie Bennett Brown and Harry Truman were married in Seattle on September 4, 1935.

It was not an easy marriage. Marge was a short, robust woman whose dark eyes flashed with jealousy when other women were around. Since there was no school at Spirit Lake, Marge's daughter Joan had to be sent to live with grandparents for nine months of the year. The separation caused Joan considerable pain and she still resents the fast-talking man she believes stole away her mother.

"I just saw my mother when they took a notion to see me," Joan Bennett Leonard now recalls. "It was a terrible experience. I disliked Harry thoroughly. I didn't feel he treated my mother well. His idea of disciplining her was to throw her in 35 feet of water in the lake. And she couldn't swim!"

Joan does retain some fond memories of the 10 summers she spent working at Spirit Lake—mainly because she became best friends with Truman's daughter Betty, who was four years older. Joan worked in the storehouse selling sundries, and Betty worked at the boat dock, renting Truman's 25 boats. Together they cleaned Truman's cabins—sometimes taking their cleaning supplies from cabin to cabin in Truman's Model A Ford. Sometimes they filled the Model A with gas and pushed it down the dirt road for a half-mile or so until they thought Truman couldn't possibly

hear them. Then the two girls would start the car and be off
on a daring jaunt up to timber line or sometimes down to
Castle Rock. Truman was inevitably angry when they returned. "One time Harry was chasing the car in his pickup
truck up the terrible winding mountain road to timber
line," Joan recalls, "and Betty went over a small cliff and
broke her thumb. It wasn't a serious accident, but Harry
was in a rage."

Joan was afraid of Truman, afraid that he'd get so angry
that he'd hit or spank them—which he never did. Betty was
better accustomed to his angry antics and just laughed them
off. Truman forbid Betty to date the Forest Service boys, but
late at night, she would sneak out of the house, climbing
down the stone fireplace from the window in the attic bedroom. One of Joan's favorite memories is of a time a man
and woman staying at the lodge had some kind of drunken
disagreement and were causing a commotion outside at 1
A.M. While Joan and Betty watched from an upstairs window, Truman walked out to investigate—wearing only his
longjohns and his hat in the bright moonlight. When he
arrived, he found the man chasing the woman in circles
around the gas pump. Both were stark naked. Truman tried
to persuade them to quiet down, but they ignored his re-
quest, and soon there were three figures circling the gas
pump—a naked man, a naked woman, and a man in a hat
and longjohns in hot pursuit.

Truman's sharp tongue and Marge's sharp temper made
for some marital battles of considerable fervor. Among the
more frequent witnesses to the confrontations were Carl
and Evelyn Forsberg of Longview. In 1936, Carl bought
Longview Ice and Storage, which included a beer franchise.
Carl remembers the first time Truman walked into the store
to buy beer, and their friendly conversation which included
Carl's inquiry about whether Truman and his wife drank.
"Oh hell yes!" came Truman's instant response. So Carl gave
Truman a bottle of Irish whiskey and soon the Forsbergs
were making frequent visits to Spirit Lake where they and

the Trumans became fast friends and drinking companions.

Hunting and fishing together were among their favorite pursuits — in season or out. One fall day, Truman and Carl went bear-hunting, and late in the afternoon they finally shot one. When they returned to the lodge, Marge had prepared a huge pot of homemade potato soup. But everyone decided to have a few drinks first, to celebrate the successful hunt, and soon Truman and Marge started an argument. "She took that kettle of potato soup and dumped it upside down right on the floor," Carl recalls. "I was so hungry I had a notion to get down on the floor and start lapping it up. Marge could be the nicest person in the world, but she also had a temper."

Carl remembers one outing in which Truman and Marge were fishing from a boat. Truman was stripping line in, letting it lie on the floor of the boat. Suddenly a big trout hit, and Truman was feeding the line with his callused hands. "Pretty soon, there was no more line, and the trout kept on going. Harry looked down to see the rest of the line lying on the floor of the boat. Marge had lit a cigarette and burned his line in two. God, Harry was mad. I think he threw Marge in the lake."

One evening in the fall of 1937, Truman and a bunch of his buddies were playing poker in the storehouse, while Marge looked on. Truman had built a big fire in his log home next door to keep it warm. Somehow, a log had rolled out of the fireplace, right onto the bear rug on the floor. By the time the poker players noticed, the log home was an inferno and no one could do anything other than watch the place burn. Marge dropped to her knees sobbing.

Later that winter, Truman caught pneumonia and had to be carried on a stretcher down to the snow line on the highway where the cars were kept parked. His recuperation period, however, gave him plenty of time to think about how to rebuild his resort and expand his business. He was sure there was more money to be made and he was determined to make it. The next winter, Truman drove down to the town of Toutle to see his builder friend, Harry Gardner. Truman patiently explained the new lodge he had in mind—complete with fancy gables and a long front porch—and he asked Gardner if he would build it. Gardner, a thoughtful man, mulled over Truman's offer and then said, "Well, I'll build you a model and you can come down and see if it's what you want." Gardner spent two weeks drawing plans and constructing a cardboard model in his living room. When Truman returned, he pranced around the model with a broad smile spreading across his face. "By God!" he said, "That's just the way I want it!"

The sounds of hammers and saws resounded at Spirit Lake in the spring of 1939. The new lodge was under construction for almost three months. Several new cabins were being built, too, by a most unusual three-man work crew. First was Joe Massey, a master carpenter and craftsman who could nail with either hand. Massey was probably one of the best-known loggers in the area because of his ability to drink heroic amounts of liquor while doing legendary amounts of work. There was also Truman, who was blessed with stamina and a determination not to let anyone outwork him or appear to outdrink him. And there was Gardner, a fanatically religious man of considerable moderation. People were always shaking their heads, asking Gardner how he could possibly work with the likes of Joe Massey and Harry Truman. "I only judge a man three ways," Gardner responded. "One is if he is on time; two is if he keeps his word; three is if he pays his bills. Truman and Massey do all of those things, so I think they're pretty good people."

Building the lodge that spring was not an easy task. It was particularly cold and wet, and it was difficult to get the hand-mixed concrete to set. The lumber had to be hauled from town. But the three workers had some great times together. There was the satisfaction that came from a long day's work and the growing recognition of how much better and bigger Truman's resort would be. Gardner enjoyed the

These earliest photographs of Truman were taken in 1916 by
"Dude" McDonell. At top: Truman shared the back seat of
a roadster with Dude's sister Mary, who is also with him in
the photograph above. (*Courtesy of Bernadette A. Mullooly.*)
At right: A picture Dude took after talking Truman into
dressing like a girl. (*Courtesy of Bernadette A. Mullooly.*)

At top: Truman's graduation from Mossyrock High School in 1917 was documented
by this photograph of his entire seven-
member class. (*Courtesy of Mossyrock High
School.*) At left: A snapshot Truman mailed
to Dude McDonell from England, where he
had been sent as an Army Air Corps mechanic. His uniform hat, he wrote her, was
lost in the shipwreck of his troop transport.
(*Courtesy of Bernadette A. Mullooly.*)

At top: During the 1930s, Truman and Verne Dickey regularly flew in and out of Spirit Lake, on fishing and hunting trips,
and —during prohibition—on bootlegging runs. (*Courtesy of
Joan Leonard.*) Above: A publicity postcard, showing the
snowed-in lodge. Truman's dog Boy is in front of the sign. At
right: Truman and his second wife, Marjorie Bennett Brown.
(*Courtesy of Joan Leonard.*)

At left: Taken in 1947, shortly after Truman and Eddie were married. (*Courtesy of Esther Burke.*) At top: Eddie posed for Truman, who included his dog Boy and cat Gilbert in the snapshot. (*Courtesy of Shirley Rosen collection.*) Above: Truman gave a hug to his "best damned boat boy," author Shirley Rosen. (*Courtesy of Shirley Rosen collection.*)

At top left: During his 1953 visit, Justice Douglas rode into the back country for five days with Truman and game warden Chickaloon Lund, who took this picture. (*Courtesy of Margaret Lund.*) Above: A rare image of Truman in a necktie, aboard the Canadian Pacific train with Eddie. (*Courtesy of Art and Nadine Clarkson.*) At left: Truman and Chickaloon Lund, mugging for Eddie on the steps of the lodge. (*Courtesy of Margaret Lund.*)

After Mount St. Helens came to life in March of 1980, Truman began to entertain newspaper reporters and photographers, including Longview's Roger Werth, who captured the 83-year-old man with his wall of mementos (top), his favorite cat (left) and his player piano. Truman's Coke glass was nearly always at hand. (*All photographs © Roger Werth*, Daily News of Longview.)

At top: For the few who could helicopter in, Truman frequently held court on the front steps of his empty lodge, which was well within the state's prohibited "Red Zone." (*Photograph © Roger Werth*, Daily News of Longview.) Above: He was apprehensive about leaving the lodge unguarded, although he did travel to Salem, Oregon, to talk to schoolchildren — just four days before the May 18th eruption. (*Courtesy of Wide World.*)

Truman's 16 cats kept him company and helped divert his attention from the incessant earthquakes, which he admitted frightened him. His other diversion was Schenley's whiskey and Coke, his favorite drink until his death. (*Both photographs* © *Roger Werth, Daily News of Longview.*)

work so much that he stayed up at the lake for more than two months.

This caused his wife Bertha endless concern. She was afraid he was being corrupted by Massey and Truman. The last time she had seen her husband drunk was several years earlier. He had taken off for the town of Winlock with a logger named P.M. Francisco and had returned sometime later with 12 puppies. She supposed the same thing could be happening up at Spirit Lake, so she finally went to fetch Gardner and bring him home. By that time, almost all the work was finished, and even Bertha Gardner had to marvel at what the three men had wrought.

6:

War and Peace

Spirit Lake was often packed on weekends in the 1940s, and a world war on two continents couldn't have seemed further away. A patriotic veteran, Truman followed the war carefully in his voracious reading of newspapers, but when the sun shone on Spirit Lake and the snowy slopes of Mount St. Helens glistened, things seemed like always—or even better. Truman's new lodge and new cabins pulled in customers anxious for an escape to a place like that, far from the headlines and radio reports of battles and dying. Truman's resort was also known as a place where one could buy booze. Truman loved his country and was loyal, but he did not see a limitation on how much liquor he bought and sold as having anything to do with his patriotism. It didn't matter that Prohibition had ended in 1933. There were new blue laws in its place in Washington State. Buying liquor required a license. Women couldn't sit at a bar. No one could stand or walk around with a drink in hand. Liquor stores closed promptly at 6 P.M., and no liquor could be sold on Sundays. All places—even bottle clubs where set-ups were sold—had to close at midnight. Such laws were simply made to be broken, Truman thought. And if one could break them and make some money, too, so much the better. He usually charged customers double what he paid for liquor.

54

Friend Carl Forsberg would load up his beer truck in Longview on Sunday mornings, when the liquor laws said deliveries could only be made between 6 A.M. and 8 A.M. At a time when some customers were being rationed beer, he'd deliver 200 cases to Truman. Cy Jacques would help Truman sell the brew. "There were so many people," Cy recalls, "that all we could sell was four quarts per person. We just didn't have enough for everybody." Beer was the only alcohol Truman had a license to sell at the lodge, but Cy can remember him "still selling moonshine and whiskey way into the '40s, if you knew him."

All sale of liquor was supposed to be suspended at midnight, but Truman was not about to have a clock regulate when he could make money. When that hour came, Truman simply locked the front doors of the lodge, pulled the plugs on the beer signs, and turned out half the lights. Everyone stayed for a night-long "private party," with drinking and dancing until 4 A.M. And many remember how they'd hear Truman outside working and whistling at 6 A.M. and they'd shake their foggy heads and wonder how the hell he did it.

The war did put one crimp in Truman's bootlegging business. For years, he had flown to Canada in a Taylor Craft seaplane to make pickups of liquor—legendary trips with Verne Dickey. Truman's seaplane jaunts were stop-and-go affairs. He was always landing at little lakes where he had hidden secret caches of gasoline. It made no difference to Truman if lakes were on Indian reservations, especially if he felt like a little fishing. He always carried the badge which made it look as if he was with the U.S. Government or the Washington State Game Department. "Truman would flash the badge and tell the Indians that he was there doing a fish census," friend Chuck Tonn recalled. "He would catch those big trout, put them in the pontoons and fly back to Spirit Lake, and cook them up, or sell them to his guests."

Taking off and landing the seaplane on isolated little lakes in the wilderness was a tricky and sometimes terrifying business, especially when the plane was loaded with cases of liquor. Because Spirit Lake was at 3,200 feet, takeoffs were always difficult, and Truman had to use the full length of the lake to coax the airplane into the thin mountain air. There were close calls.

Truman and his brother-in-law Buck Whiting (who'd married Truman's sister Geri in 1935) ran out of gas once on their way home from a fishing trip to Horsefly Lake in British Columbia, 240 miles north of the border. They made a dead-stick landing on a tiny lake that was nearby, and then went ashore to buy gas. But when they had filled the tank with gas, the plane was too heavy and the lake too short for take-off with two people. Truman had to hire a ride overland to a larger lake where Whiting could land and take off with both of them aboard. And even routine journeys were hardly uneventful; on trips to Canada, Truman would load the plane with rocks and drop them on moose as he flew overhead.

World War II grounded the Taylor Craft seaplane and ended the escapades on the liquor runs to Canada. Truman was sure the plane would be confiscated. There were severe restrictions on flying, and aviation gas was almost impossible to buy. So Truman dismantled the seaplane and stashed it in a garage, he later told Chuck Tonn.

The war brought other restrictions, too. Fears of fires and sabotage caused the national forests to become off limits for all but a few people. Visitors to Truman's resort had to stay right by the lake and couldn't travel the trails into the back country at all. Even Weyerhaeuser logging crews were limited by the strict security.

Truman bristled at the restrictions. He considered the wilderness around Spirit Lake and Mount St. Helens to be "my wilderness" and he frequently trekked into the back country alone—refreshing his spirit. So when "my wilderness" became off limits during the war, Truman knew he had to find a way around the restrictions and of course he did—as he usually did with restrictions. Truman simply waited and watched for a Forest Service mule pack train to come out of the back country. Then he would go to town and buy some steaks and two or three bottles of whiskey and go to the Spirit Lake Forest Service headquarters and volunteer to pack in some food for "the boys." They would give him a government mule—anyone in the woods without one was considered to be there illegally—and Truman would take off. His saddle packs usually contained more whiskey than food. After dropping off supplies to the men, Truman would roam the woods and mountains alone for two or three days—drinking and eating and fishing—and then return to Spirit Lake restored and refreshed.

Getting around poaching restrictions took far less effort for Truman, since he'd been doing it practically from the first day he arrived at Spirit Lake. It was a cat-and-mouse game that Truman played with a series of game wardens year after year. Bill Hall was the warden at Spirit Lake from 1935 to 1941 and he tried every trick he could think of to catch Truman. He would head into the woods for a week at a time hunting poachers—sleeping on the forest floor by smoking campfires—and when he came back out all he would have to show for his efforts would be a face full of whiskers. Hall even found Truman's cave above Spirit Lake; he called it "Harry's meat cellar." "The meat hooks were there and I knew that's where Truman was stashing it," he recalls. "But every time I got up there, there'd be nothing. I stayed up many a night lying in the woods watching for him to put some meat in the cave, but I never did catch him doing it. It wasn't that we didn't try to catch Harry. He was just too slick."

Hall never caught Truman fishing out of season, either. But he believed Truman was particularly careful about fishing because he didn't want to jeopardize his fishing license dealership, which would have jeopardized his boat business. Truman received a commission of 25 cents on every fishing license he sold, and he sold hundreds. Many fishermen came to Spirit Lake carrying Cowlitz County fishing licenses. But Spirit Lake was four miles inside the Skamania

County line and Cowlitz licenses weren't valid. When Hall and other game wardens caught unsuspecting fishermen at Spirit Lake who had the wrong county licenses, they advised: "You go down to Harry Truman's and buy a Skamania County license." Most fishermen did just that. In exchange for the license business which the game wardens sent his way, Truman kept records of the number of fishermen and how many had caught their limits. Truman also kept track of where the fish were biting and what bait was being used. He shared that information with the game wardens, who passed it to *The Daily News* of Longview.

Bill Hall's successor during World War II, Guy Burnham, was responsible for Truman's first and only poaching citation. It involved not an elk, or a deer, or a moose; the poaching case involved canned venison. Burnham somehow found out that Truman and Marge kept jars of venison neatly stacked on shelves in the basement of the lodge. Regulations required that all deer killed during the hunting season, which began in mid-October, had to be eaten before August 1 of the following year. Since it was past that date when the warden discovered the venison in the cellar, Truman was ticketed. Worse yet, Truman's lawyer insisted he give all the canned meat to a home for girls in Chehalis.

Truman never made that mistake again. Each year when August approached, he would move any remaining canned venison from the cellar to the second floor of the lodge where he would hide it there behind removable wall panels. After it had been there for a while, Truman would get worried and move the venison again—to the third-floor crow's nest, where there was storage space under loose floor boards.

Once Truman's poaching earned him a place of honor at the head table of a banquet and the chance to meet Jack Dempsey. During World War II, the famed former heavyweight boxing champion crisscrossed the country selling war bonds. In June, 1943, Dempsey came to Longview and Kelso, neighboring cities across the Cowlitz River. Max

Eckenbeck of the Kelso Elks Club was in charge of arrangements. There was to be a banquet dinner honoring Dempsey, and Eckenbeck wanted to serve venison, a main course Dempsey wasn't likely to see at the many banquets. One evening Eckenbeck spotted Harry Truman and Carl Forsberg sitting at the Elks Club bar, "getting pretty well organized." Thoughts started to click quickly in his head —here was the poacher of countywide reputation, and here was the owner of Longview Ice and Storage, with meat lockers where game could be kept frozen.

"I know that you fellows are pretty good hunters," Eckenbeck said to the two. "We would like to put on a venison dinner for Jack Dempsey and I was wondering if you have any meat left from last fall?" With scarcely a pause, Carl responded, "Yeah, I've got a lot of it in my locker."

As Eckenbeck may have suspected, he didn't. That evening Carl and Truman took off for the woods in search of some "frozen venison." Working along the chilly North Toutle, they used spotlights and shot two deer, dressed them and put the meat in Carl's cold-storage plant. "We didn't want any fresh venison showing up," Carl recalls. "So we froze them." The banquet was a smashing success, particularly the venison. At one point Eckenbeck took Carl aside and said, "Carl, I've eaten a lot of venison in my life and those haven't been frozen very long, have they?" Carl just smiled. He and Truman were sitting at the head table with Dempsey, the liquor was flowing, and they were all having a hell of a good time. Carl enjoyed himself so much, in fact, that by the end of the evening he had somehow bought war bonds worth $70,000.

Truman's personal life was far less cheerful. His marriage to Marge was turning even rockier. Her daughter Joan had married, moved to California and was about to have her first baby in 1944. Marge left to be there when the baby was born. "That's when the marriage started going to pieces," Joan Leonard remembers. "She stayed too long. Harry didn't want her down there; he wanted her up at the lake."

Their separation lengthened and that same summer the two sisters from Seattle arrived on the bus at Castle Rock. He started courting my mother that fall, then later switched to Auntie Eddie. She was separated from her husband in August, 1945. Nine months later, and now divorced, she took another vacation to Spirit Lake. Eddie ended up staying and falling in love with Truman. "And Harry worshipped Eddie," remembers friend George Bowers.

Truman and Eddie would tell her family that they were married in the fall of 1946 in Stevenson, Washington. But actually they were living together then and he was in the process of petitioning for a divorce from Marge. A Lewis County Court document explained: "Their temperaments are so incompatible they cannot longer live together; longer life of plaintiff with the defendant is burdensome to him."

Marge would not have divorced Truman, even though she knew about Eddie. She still loved him. "Mother always thought they would get back together," remembers Joan Leonard. Marge's vain hopes of a reconciliation were so strong, Joan recalls, that she left all her personal possessions at Spirit Lake packed in trunks in the attic of the boathouse.

The divorce was granted in early 1947 and on September 11 of that year, Truman was married for a third time. It was a quiet wedding with no family invited, and it was performed by Skamania County Justice of the Peace Cleo Brown.

Marge Truman died seven years later, when she was only 53 years old. Her death was caused, her daughter would come to believe, by a broken heart.

Truman himself had never been happier. He was in love, his namesake was now President and his resort business was booming.

7:

A Diary and a Distinguished Visitor

THE years following World War II would prove to be Truman's happiest and most profitable. Truman and Eddie truly loved one another and their love was so joyous and so full of kidding that they were a pleasure to be around. Even Truman's rough edges sometimes seemed smoothed.

Truman and Eddie did everything together. He often took her over the back-country trails by horseback, up along the ridges and into the rugged mountain meadows he loved. She delighted in their trips together and shared his appreciation for the seclusion of the wilderness.

The people who came to know the two of them well, believed that Eddie was the strength behind the man—a selfless giver of her love and support who knew just when to let Truman rumble and just when to cut him off. "Truman," she would say, "go suck an egg."

"She was the boss," recalls Chuck Tonn of the Forest Service. "It was real obvious and yet she was a lady, a great woman." "She was a beautiful woman to look at," remembers Jim Lund, the son of game warden Chickaloon Lund, "but she was a helluva lot more beautiful from the heart, too. Why, Harry Truman would never have survived if it weren't for Eddie. I think she's the one who pulled him through; he didn't do it. I think he would have poisoned his own self in time from just being ornery."

Eddie even seemed to enjoy the long dark winters at Spirit Lake when few people were around and the weather made it a constant struggle to survive. She kept a daily diary during the winter of 1949—a brutal time—and some of the entries give a picture of what life was like when they were alone in the lodge and the snowstorms kept coming one after another.

Her comments, written on blue stationary with a portable typewriter, were filled with cryptic notations, makeshift abbreviations and her own creative spelling and punctuation. January began with a cold and clear day. There were seven feet of snow on the ground around the lodge. Truman had recently purchased a Sno-Cat from two members of the Longview Ski Club and there were expectations of towing groups of skiers up to the timber line and actually making some money in the winter. But the month ended with worries about wildlife and horses and how to keep them alive as the temperature hovered near zero for much of the month.

January 1
Just Harry, Red [Hiles, Truman's hired hand and friend] and I. Roast pork dinner. 7 feet of snow. Cold and clear.
January 9
Biggest bunch of skiers yet. Kids took the place over but no money in it.
January 12
Orlie and Irene [Stingley] and us played on skis, snowshoes; out on lake. Jack [Nelson of Harmony Falls Lodge] came out with infected hand. Took movies and color pictures next day.
January 24
To Longview. Harry talked to Bill Hall [Regional Game Supervisor] about Elk situation. To Centralia to see Betty [Harry's daughter] and Harry's mother. Get new waffle iron.

January 26

Harry and Red up early to distribute some of hay for elk.

January 27

Down road again to put out more hay. Find towhead [elk] killed by coyote. Temperature up to 20 above at 2 P.M. Warmest for some three weeks. Winter has been with us since Nov. 1. 9 feet of snow.

February was even worse. The snow kept coming and so did the cold. A snowslide blocked the highway to the lodge for days. The isolation at the lodge prompted Eddie to think of spring flowers and warm weather, and she got out a road map and took an imaginary trip to the sunny southwest.

February 8

Seth [Cook, driver of the Highway Department snowplow which kept the road open in winter] did not come in by 11 A.M. so figured road slide. Harry and Red take snocat pulling pickup; left here at 11 A.M. Terrible blizzard.

Radio from Seattle made first report at noon about road block at Spirit Lake. Blowing so bad can't see one-half block ahead. Hope the guys find their way home. They have snow shoes so can walk home if they have to give up cat.

They got home at 5:30 P.M., dug out most of slide by shovel as pickup bogged down. After three hours were on other side. Left snocat and [went] rest of the way in pickup; Seth couldn't believe his eyes when he saw them. Met rotary plow on way in but will be three days or more before they get through slide and these heavy drifts. Horses in good shape.

February 10

Thawed during nite, icicles & snow falling off roof. Colder this morning and wind strong, snowing. Floods and slides in Oregon due to heavy rains and melting snow. Sam [Forest Ranger Harold Samuelson] in. [His home] is completely snowed under. Had to dig down four feet [to get into the house]. The threat of floods is here unless rain falls off below.

Harry and Red came back without pickup. Left it at Langes' after stopped by slide below there and another further on. Took snocat down this afternoon to see if snow plows making any headway. May be several days before we can get out. Wind stopped blowing, seems to be clearing up. Boys took me down to see slide. Blower well into first one. Slide at Langes' is 6 feet deep and 200 feet [wide]; lower one is 12 feet by 300 feet.

February 11

Water went out on us about 9 o'clock last nite. They went to dam this morning to see if trouble could be there. If not, pipe has broken under lake. In that case, we will be without water until lake opens up again, probably three or four months from now. Melting snow in pans for dishes and water from spring for cooking and drinking. At least we can leave here without worry of pipes etc. freezing up.

Managed to live through one [day] without water coming in the pipes. Must limit nature's call to once a day. Made Judy [Truman's grandaughter] a pinafore apron without benefit of measurements and by hand. First time I ever did that.

February 13

Harry went out yesterday to get groceries and rubber hose to remake temporary water system. Mail from my folks and the Wallaces. No cars or skiers in this weekend because of road block.

Oh yes, got a Valentine box of candy from my boy-friend. Rotary [snowplow] in at 1 P.M. Hope they get done today. Boys went down to feed horses and elk. Snowing. Down to zero last night.

February 17

Boys off to town at 8:30 in snowcat. Rained all nite.

Then turned to snow early this morning and snowed ever since. Hope no more til they get safely home.

After four months of winter, begins to get very tiresome. Start to wish for spring. Last nite dreamed of flowers bursting into bloom. Also new white stucco house with red trim, ultra modern. Cherry trees, peonies, strawberries and a store just a step or two away where you could buy everything; one of those super duper markets. What a dream! sun shining and so nice and warm.

Have to get busy on this living room. Soot all over from blowing down chimney. They got back at 2 P.M. Guys back shoveling snow. Awfully heavy on cabins after rain. Maintenance shed caved in at gate.

February 21

Four inches [of snow] last nite. Trying to thaw. Big sloppy flakes. Our road wide and clean. Got most of cabins [cleaned] on one side. Will take a week to get caught up again.

Took a trip via road map to Death Valley and Vegas to get some sun. Ended up going to Albuquerque, El Paso, San Antonio, New Orleans and all the National Parks in New Mexico, Arizona and Utah. Some fun dreaming.

February 22

Boy got in a fight with a beaver and badly chewed up on both shoulders.

February 24

Took Boy to the vet. Shaved and painted him.

February 28

Make bread, guys dug out a couple cabins. First time in them since elk season and in pretty fair shape. Work on light lines. Go and get wood. Boat house floating again.

March was a month for digging out, cleaning up, and taking stock of the damage that winter had brought. But as the snow melted, the roads were opened and travel to the lowlands became easier and more frequent. Truman and Eddie took trips to his old place at Cowlitz Falls, to their Airstream trailer near Longview, and to the Washington coast town of Long Beach. Every time they returned to the lodge, there was more work to be done. Winter's grip was far from gone.

March 5
Ski party this eve. Serve sandwiches and chili. Eight stayed in lodge. Few breakfasts.

March 19
Doc Christy and friends wake us up at 6 A.M. for cabin 5. They walked 10 miles. Flat tire. Red [Hiles] went down, picked up the women and got them settled. Make chili and pie, clean house. Skiers start coming in at noon. About 20 for party.

March 21
Clean up debris from yesterday, laundry, wash, etc. Boys go down to saw wood. Snowed couple inches last nite and still snowing. Hope it quits or will spoil our plans for trip to south and sun.

Think I'll get some flower seeds and start in boxes down in the orchard as soon as it warms up, then take them up here later in the summer. If we have some. Still 6 feet of snow.

March 26
Up late. More snow and cold as heck. Down to wood and bring home load. Blizzard now. Letter from Shirley [me, then 15] and Mom. Got to catch up on correspondence. Several behind. Bake and clean up for weekend.

March 27
Go to town at noon. Harry cleans station wagon. Ride around Longview. Chicken dinner, show. At Carls [Forsberg] for awhile. Orlie and Irene [Stingley] there.

Back to trailer. Sleep there overnite.

March 30

My birthday. Mom sent me pair of nylons. Snowed 6 inches last nite. Moderately at noon. To town in pickup. Send Seth to plow us out. Get gas and oil. Gifts and cards from Jerry, Esther, Betty, Mom B. Home early.

April was the time for escape, a three-week trip to Las Vegas. Truman and Eddie often took winter trips to warm places south: Las Vegas, Reno, Phoenix, Tucson, and Mexico. The trips were a welcome respite from the snows and the cold, and a rest before the frantic preparations for re-opening the resort. The trip also provided Eddie with a three-week vacation from her diary writing.

April 1

Phoned Las Vegas last nite. Got our reservations for kitchenette. Probably leave here the 4th if luck and the weather with us. Oh, yes. Truman had tooth pulled. Major operation.

April 23

Have a cocktail with Mr. & Mrs. Veys at new Castle Rock bar. Not quite finished. Get mail and groceries, unpack station wagon, off for home at 7 P.M. Red [Hiles], Frank [Wilkinson], Bill [Snaza] home. Sleeping by fireplace since earthquake—some figurines broken, bottles knocked over and radio off bed table. Nothin serious. Thank G[od].

April 24

Sunshine—lots of cars up—could rent boats if lake were open. Clean house. Patch chimney. Go down to orchard and play with horses awhile. Full of pep and nonsense.

April 26

Clean and scrub all day. Check cabins—no quake damage, not one dish broken. Red and Truman work

on boat dock, light lines. Coast guard in asking about
missing plane.

May was the month for the final sprucing up. Painting the
kitchen began on the first of the month and seemed to take
days. It was a frantic time full of work and Eddie stopped
trying to keep up her diary after May 11. The customers
were coming soon.

May 5
Paint kitchen. Start bathroom. Men move boat
house. Take shakes off cabin porches. Fix door locks.
Shave doors and cupboards.

May 7
Clean up apartment [their living quarters] and
shampoo. First time since left Vegas. Paint red on windows outside. Down to orchard in eve. Apple trees in
bloom. Letter from Esther. Also reservations pouring
in for Memorial Day weekend.

May 8
Frank and I paint doors and cupboards, shelves in
cabins 11, 13, 14, 15, 16. Finish first coat on lodge windows. Orchard for evening ride.
At least 200 cars up. Beautiful day. Red breaks thru
ice on lake. Warm east wind helps. Will have to work
like mad to open for next weekend.

May 11
Clean out office desk, give it a paint job. Also paint
more doors, cabins. To orchard, plant Richfield wild
flower seeds. Harry half finished roof of lodge in front.
Looks marvelous.

I arrived a few weeks after that to begin my second
summer of working at Spirit Lake for Truman and Auntie
Eddie. I was 15. I remember seeing the baby colt that had
been born that spring and how cute it was when I arrived
and how sad we all were when it was stolen later in the
summer. Truman was furious.

There was a different kind of sadness and anger the following summer, my last at Spirit Lake. I vividly remember sitting in the kitchen listening to the radio on June 27, 1950. President Truman announced he was ordering United States air and naval forces to provide support to the South Koreans, who had been invaded by North Korea the previous Sunday. "Oh my God," Truman said, shaking his head, "not another war." President Truman continued his explanation. Our forces would be joining those of the United Nations for the first time in history.

Uncle Truman paced the kitchen with his arms swinging at his sides. He was growing angrier by the minute. "He's right, goddamnit, the President's right." He fairly spit the words across the room. "You can't let those sons-a-bitchin' Red Commies get away with it. The goddamn Russians are behind it. Those bastards want to rule the whole goddamn world." Auntie Eddie tried to soothe him. "Now calm down, Truman," she said. "You're going to bust your gizzard."

Truman proudly put out the two large American flags which he usually displayed only on holidays. As we listened to the distorted voices on the radio, Truman constantly tinkered with the antenna trying to clear the static which interrupted the reception. He met everyone who came in the lodge that day, bombarding them with questions about the war and asking whether they had a current newspaper. Truman had always been an avid newspaper reader. He subscribed to the Portland *Oregonian* and several smaller papers as well. He instructed us to save any magazines we found cleaning the cabins and bring them to the lodge so he could read them. And whenever friends came to visit, they inevitably brought Truman a bottle of Schenley's whiskey—his favorite—and a newspaper. If they only brought the bottle, Truman would snap, "Well, where in the hell is my newspaper?" That summer of 1950, the avid newspaper reader turned into a newspaper-reading fanatic. Truman, the World War I veteran, followed the Korean War intently—in part, perhaps, because the Commander in Chief was named Harry Truman.

"The commies" gave Truman someone to complain about besides the Republicans. Throughout his life, he blamed the Republicans for bad weather, bad business, high taxes, poor booze, and full outhouses. It was the Republicans' fault, as far as he was concerned, when Auntie Eddie got mad at him. The Republicans were even to blame for the hordes who later crowded the Spirit Lake campground instead of his lodge. "The only reason people stay in the campground," he'd say, "is because the goddamn Republicans have the taxes too high and people can't afford to rent a cabin from ol' Truman."

That summer of 1950 was also one of some personal upheaval at Spirit Lake. First, Truman got into a terrible fight with his helper Red Hiles—which was not an uncommon occurrence, except this time Red was drunk and he was meaner then. Red had Truman down by the neck and Auntie Eddie was sure he was going to kill Truman so she grabbed a rifle and hit Red over the head. It knocked him cold, and broke the rifle stock, too. Red was a hard worker and had helped Truman through more than one brutal winter. But a couple of weeks later, Truman accused Red of stealing, and sent him packing with the words: "Get the hell off my place and never come back!" A few years later, all was forgiven and Red returned.

Truman had counted on the help of Bill Snaza, who had been with him for seven years, and the newly hired Bill Dougherty. But the two Bills were soon in trouble, too. When Truman had gone to town one day, they decided to do a little fishing with what Dougherty called "DuPont spinners"—sticks of dynamite. So they helped themselves to Truman's supply and proceeded to drop a stick of dynamite into the water where Spirit Lake flowed into the Toutle River.

"There was a varoom!" Snaza recalls. "Then here came suckers, little trout and everything flying out of the river. The next thing that came along was Eddie. She had a kitchen knife in her hand and she was mad. I thought she was going to kill us both."

After cleaning up all the dead fish, the two Bills beat a strategic retreat—hiking into the back country for a few days. When they returned, Truman confronted them, wanting to know where they had been and when they were going to get back to work. They decided to quit instead—which they did on the spot.

Truman solved his labor problem by drafting me, from cabin cleaning to supervising the boat dock. He taught me how to fill the motors with gas, how to prime and start them. He reminded me to be sure that every boat always had a full gallon of gas in the bow. And he showed me how to keep track of time and where to keep the money. Truman had about 40 boats. Johnson outboards were $2.50 an hour, rowboats were $2.50 a day and canoes were $1 an hour. I enjoyed working with the boats and was proud because people seemed to be surprised when the boat dock was being run by a girl. I was even prouder when I'd hear Truman say, "Goddamn go to hell if she isn't the cutest, sharpest boat 'boy' I've ever had! I'll be goddamned if I'm not making more money and the records aren't kept better, too."

The loss of Snaza was keenly felt at the lodge. Snaza was a dependable hard worker whose seven years there had been a time of great growth—including the construction of some 14 new cabins. And Snaza worked for the pittance paid by Truman—$50 a month plus free room and board—whether he was splitting shakes, building new cabins, or running the boat dock. Truman recognized Snaza's contributions and tried to convince him to return to work. But Snaza decided to stay away the rest of that summer, even though he and Truman remained close.

"Harry was really good to me," Snaza recalls. "He never gave me a bad time." One of Snaza's most vivid memories is of a boat customer who tried to leave without paying. Snaza called for Truman, who caught up to the man at the gas pump. "The guy was giving Harry a bunch of lip," Snaza recalls, "so ol' Harry bopped him one, and there was ol' Boy, his dog, chewin' right on the guy's ankle, too. Harry had the guy on the ground and the guy finally said, 'Well get your dog off me and maybe I could do something about paying.'"

Boy's toughness and showmanship were a carbon copy of Truman's, and it was hard to tell which of the two considered himself more of an institution at Spirit Lake. Both took the role very seriously. Boy would pose whenever photographers came around. Boy would ride to town with Truman in his pickup and would always want to accompany him on his rounds; if Truman didn't let him out of the truck, Boy would sit and pout all the way back to Spirit Lake.

Once Truman lost Boy on a trip back from buying groceries. Instead of his usual spot in the passenger seat, the dog was sitting on a load of beer in the back of the pickup. Truman was driving the way he always did on the Spirit Lake Highway—fast—and as he rounded a curve, Boy was flipped right off the truck. Truman was shaken when he returned to the lodge, telling Snaza, "By God, I just killed my dog." But when Truman went back down the road to look for his body, Boy was heading home up the highway as if nothing had happened. "That dog was just like Harry," says Snaza.

Truman had more than his share of accidents and injuries himself. Once, he was shoveling snow off the roof of the boathouse when he slipped and went flying right through the ice into the lake. Another time, he dropped a motor on his foot and mashed it. He once got so mad at the generator that wouldn't start that he kicked it and broke his big toe. Another time, he was chopping wood and the ax head flew off and hit him square in the head. He was bleeding profusely and everyone wanted to take him to the doctor but Truman manfully refused. "Just pour a little of that hydrogen peroxide in the gash," he said, "and put some Band-aids on real tight. Can't go running to town for every goddamn little cut."

Truman had far more faith in his own home remedies than he did in doctors. He kept his favorites in a small cabinet with sliding doors which he installed next to the kitchen sink. There was Alka Seltzer, aspirin, Ben-Gay, hydrogen peroxide, rubbing alcohol and of course Absorbine Junior. That pungent green liquid with the distinctive sting was his old stand-by remedy, capable of curing just about any ailment. And Truman never kept just one bottle or package of anything—if one was good, two were better and three were better still. He usually had at least four bottles of Absorbine Junior.

Absorbine Junior was what Truman often applied to his sore feet, caused by his being on his feet all day. Truman would often sit down in his favorite chair in front of the gas heater and take off his shoes and socks. "Goddamn," he'd say, "my feet are sore." Then he'd rub them down with Absorbine Junior. Truman changed his shoes two or three times a day. He'd start the day with ankle-high work boots, then switch at noontime to the navy blue tennis shoes with the holes in them. Late in the day he'd switch to sandals with white socks, or slippers. The rest of his clothes stayed pretty constant—cotton chino pants and a long-sleeve sport shirt and an old sweatshirt. It was only on trips that he would pull out his best slacks and his plaid Pendleton shirts.

One of Truman's more spectacular spills occurred on a back-country pack trip with Carl Forsberg. Carl and Evelyn Forsberg had been friends of Harry and Marge Truman, but they became better friends when he married Eddie, and the four took winter trips to California, Arizona, and Nevada. Evelyn and Eddie would often stay at the lodge while Carl and Harry trekked off on fishing trips.

Truman saddled up Tony, his black stallion, and Carl saddled up Donut, his Tennessee walker, and they headed off. The sky was cloudless and the sun was bright. The huckleberries were ripe in the back country and Truman had put a couple pints of fresh cream in the pack boxes on his mule, along with his fishing gear, in anticipation of a dinner of fresh trout and huckleberries with cream for dessert. The only sound which disturbed the quiet—besides Truman's occasional chatter—was the muffled thumping of the horses' hoofs on the trail. That sound turned to a grating staccato as the trail turned to volcanic pumice in the high country. They headed through the section of Independence Pass where the trail narrows and there is a steep drop off the lower side of the trail. That is exactly where Truman's horse began bucking.

"Instead of Harry falling off on the upper side of the trail," Carl recalls, "he went flying into the air on the lower side of the trail toward the canyon. He was spread-eagled and I bet he went 40 feet. He lit into the jack firs down there, where he finally came to a halt. Then he came back up the slope slowly—bruised and hurting a little—cussed Tony out, climbed back into the saddle and continued the trip."

One morning the two men walked into the hills in search of huckleberries when they encountered a black bear mother and her cub. The mother backed into the brush woofing and growling; the cub scampered up a tree. "Let's go back to camp and get an ax and cut that tree down," said Truman excitedly, "then capture the cub and wrap it in a blanket. Then we could take it back to the lake. I'd like to have him there for a tourist attraction."

Carl was aghast. They were 25 miles from Spirit Lake, an all-day trip at least, and here was Truman proposing to kidnap a bear cub in plain sight of its mother. "You must be out of your mind, Truman," Carl exclaimed. "The mother bear isn't going to like that, and if you get that cub on the horse, the horse isn't going to like it, either. We're going to have nothing but trouble." Truman wasn't totally convinced, and it took quite some persuading before Carl finally prevailed.

The relationship between the Trumans and the Forsbergs was not without a few strains every now and then. Once Truman had asked Evelyn to help with the crowds over the Fourth of July holiday and she had agreed, little knowing how hard the work—without pay—would be. She helped get her own meals, waited on customers and helped clean, and when she ran out of cigarettes towards the end of her stay, she went behind the counter and got a carton of Luckies. Then she kiddingly offered to pay Truman for them. To her bone-weary amazement, he put the money in the till. For the first time, she saw the difference between the generous Truman she saw on winter vacation trips and the all-business character running the resort in the summer.

Those of us Lapham nieces who worked summers at the lodge often saw the same thing. Truman could be gruff, blustery and downright ornery to people in the summers. He thought nothing of turning away customers with reservations if they made the mistake of bringing a boat—thus depriving Truman of his chance to make money on his boats. He would turn away others because he simply didn't like the way they looked or talked. That happened in the summer of 1953, when Truman turned away the man who would become the lodge's most famous guest.

My sister Elaine was on duty in the lodge when the middle-aged man walked in. He was wearing a rumpled suit, his tie was askew, and he had a squashed hat on his head. He looked like just another fisherman to Elaine. Truman, who was sitting by the door in the kitchen, eyed the man with obvious disapproval as he walked around the interior of the lodge.

Truman motioned to Elaine. "Hey, kid," he said, "go out there in the lobby and tell that old coot that if he wants a cabin, we don't have any. Tell him we're all full up." Elaine did as she was told. She walked over to the counter and when the man inquired about renting a cabin, she told him all the cabins were taken. She suggested he head down the road to Spirit Lake Lodge. A half-dozen men were sitting at the counter drinking beers and after a few minutes one of them yelled over to Truman, "Hey, Truman, do you know who that was that you just turned away? That was Supreme Court Justice William O. Douglas!"

"I'll be goddamn go to hell!" Truman shouted. He shot out the back door, jumped in his pickup, and sped down the road. By the time he caught up with Douglas, the justice was inside the Spirit Lake Lodge, a rustic log building on the edge of the fast-flowing Toutle a mile down the road. Douglas was in the process of registering. The owners, Harry and Emma Gustafson, were away, but a young couple was manning the front desk, and they watched with amazement as Truman blew through the front door and descended upon Douglas, his mouth moving at full Truman speed. Truman apologized and explained that some mistake had been made. "That niece of my wife's doesn't know a goddamn thing about what's going on," he said. "She doesn't know shit. We don't have a cabin vacant now, but we do have a nice room up in the lodge you can have. And I've got some great horses." Douglas's ears perked up at the mention of the horses; he had been hoping to take a horseback trip into the back country. So he apologized to the young couple at the desk and followed Truman back to his lodge.

Justice Douglas had returned that summer to his beloved Washington State to seek solice and peace in the wilderness, as he often did. But that summer he had a special need for the perspective that nature gave him. Only a few weeks before, Douglas had stayed the execution of Julius and Ethel Rosenburg, the couple convicted of selling atomic secrets to the Russians. Douglas's action on June 17 had prompted angry comment in Congress and a Georgia representative had introduced a resolution to impeach him. Douglas was used to controversy, but he was deeply disturbed and saddened when the full Supreme Court lifted his stay two days later on a six-to-three vote and the Rosenburgs were electrocuted that night at Sing Sing prison—the first American civilians ever executed for espionage. Douglas later told Truman how much the Rosenburg case upset him and how wrong the decision had been and how barbaric he thought capital punishment was.

Truman was doing all he could to pamper his guest. The morning after Douglas arrived, Truman instructed Elaine, "Now as soon as the people in cabin 9 check out, you hightail it down there and clean that cabin good. Put in all new blankets, new sheets and make sure you put in new towels because that's where Justice Douglas is going to stay." That evening, Truman invited Douglas to join him and Eddie for drinks and dinner in the lodge. The two lifelong Democrats got along famously during the justice's 10-day stay. Douglas saw Truman as a breath of Washington State fresh air. He could truly relax with Truman, he could be himself. Truman responded with his "remember when" stories and his un-bridled opinions about everything and everyone. The two actually looked somewhat alike; they could have been brothers, this graduate of Whitman College in Walla Walla, Washington and Yale Law School, a Supreme Court Justice of the United States, and this graduate of Mossyrock High in Mossyrock, Washington, this self-made man who was turning a resort in the wilderness into a million-dollar busi-ness. Their ages were similar—Truman was just two years older—and the two had grown up and gone to school less than 100 miles apart. They had more in common than they must have thought at first.

Truman and Douglas nurtured their new friendship on a five-day ride into the back country that covered more than 50 miles. They were accompanied by Truman's good friend and game warden, John "Chickaloon" Lund. Truman rode his horse Needles and Douglas rode Eddie's Patches. Tru-man began the trip with his usual outburst of modesty, telling Douglas, "There ain't no one livin' who knows that ol' mountain and the trails around it better than ol' Truman from the hills of West Virginia."

They headed up through Bear Pass, past Grizzly Lake, Boot Lake, Obscurity Lake and Panhandle Lake. They stopped at many of the abandoned mines which are an important part of the pioneer history of the area—Polar Star, Last Hope, and Black Prince. Truman told Douglas that the Golconda was the only gold mine of the bunch. All along the route Justice Douglas snapped pictures continu-ously and they rode on to Chickaloon's favorite fishing hole—Deadman's Lake. They fished and fried their catch

around the campfire at night. They drank, too. Truman
usually went into the wilderness well stocked, and he had
plenty of Schenley's for himself and Chickaloon, and Scotch
for Douglas. That led to long, lusty conversations and, as it
often did, a bit of an accident.

"I was just standing by the campstove yakking away,"
Truman liked to recall, "and I thought my legs were getting
a mite warm. But before I knew it, my pants were on fire."
Douglas quickly scrambled out of his sleeping bag and
smothered the fire, but Truman had severely burned both
of his calves. As usual, he rigorously refused the urgings
that he must see a doctor, even when the urgings came from
a Supreme Court Justice. Truman preferred drugstore
ointments and his own dressings.

They returned to the lodge the next day. They unpacked
their creels filled with Eastern Brook trout, each fish deli-
cately set upon a bed of huckleberry branches to cushion
the ride back to the lodge. Then Truman and Douglas sat
around out behind the lodge with Eddie, Elaine and Al
"Peg-leg" Brimsfield and someone fetched a camera and
Eddie and Douglas started snapping pictures. Truman
played his usual role as director, instructing Douglas, "Now
don't go takin' any pictures of my bad side and show my big
nose and balding head. Take all your pictures from the
front." Douglas could only oblige, just as he did around the
lodge when Truman had him chopping wood, taking trips
in the launch, and running to the dump at Coldwater.

Truman always carried his .410 sawed-off shotgun behind
the seat of the pickup, keeping a keen eye out for grouse as
he headed down the highway to the dump. He usually just
poked the gun out the window of the truck if someone else
was driving. It isn't known whether Mr. Justice Douglas was
driving that morning, or whether he offered a dissenting
opinion. What is certain, though, is that Truman pulled the
illegal gun out from behind the seat and then shot four
grouse, well out of season. Truman cleaned them and Eddie
soaked them in white wine, garlic, and water overnight and

they had them for breakfast the next day. As Eddie fried the birds in bubbling butter, a guest stuck her head through the kitchen doorway and commented, "Never thought of eating chicken for breakfast—sure smells good—how do you fix it, anyway?" Douglas, Al Brimsfield, and Elaine, their mouths full of the succulent illegal game, looked guilty as Eddie glibly responded, "With hash browns and eggs." Truman winked at Douglas and added, "And with lots of pepper."

The very next day, the justice climbed Mount St. Helens. Truman stayed behind because he had climbed the mountain plenty of times in his youth. Douglas was joined on the climb by two of his closest friends who had grown up with him in Yakima—Elon Gilbert and Dr. Douglas Corpron. Seven other climbers joined the party, which was led by Rob and Val Quoidbach of the Longview Ski Club and Bob McCall of the Mount St. Helens Ski Patrol and Search and Rescue Unit. The three were well known as the best guides on Mount St. Helens; the two Quoidbach brothers had climbed the mountain almost 200 times. Val Quoidbach still remembers the telegram which he and his brother received from Washington, D.C. just before starting out. "No matter what happens," it read, "Justice Douglas is to be taken care of first. Douglas must come off the mountain alive and well."

The Quoidbachs and McCall had not chosen the easiest route to the summit, which ran up past Dogs Head. They had instead selected the Lizard's route, which was more scenic and would provide dazzling views of the Forsythe Glacier and its crevass-studded ice fields. Douglas had donned a cowboy hat and put black grease all over his face to avoid a sunburn and he frequently stopped to take pictures. He also impressed other members of the climbing party with his knowledge of plants and flowers along the way. But the eight-hour climb to the summit took its toll on the 55-year-old justice, who had been run ragged by Truman. The two-hour trip down was slow and agonizing and

Douglas was winded. Douglas returned to Truman's lodge and stayed a couple more days, then took off to climb Gilbert Peak near Yakima.

Members of the Longview Ski Club were particularly active in the Spirit Lake area in the early 1950s and Truman and Eddie had come to consider many club members their friends. The club members had first built a cabin near the timber line on Mount St. Helens in 1938. They had installed a small rope tow on a hillside above Gustafson's Spirit Lake Lodge in the mid-1940s at a place called Woodpecker's Paradise. They decided to move the rope tow up to the timber line in 1949.

That was when visions of a booming winter business began dancing in Truman's head and he plunked down $4,000 to buy a Sno-Cat from ski club members Val Quoidbach and Ron Bascom. Truman could transport four skiers inside the cat and pull 10 more behind on ropes as he took them from the lodge up to the timber line where they would catch the rope tow and then ski down the mountain. Truman charged each person $2 for the one-way trip. He was so enthused about the prospects for the winter business that he even allowed the ski club members to hook up a telephone line between the timber line and his lodge where they hung a large sign that said: "Phone for Sno-Cat." For years, Truman was vehemently opposed to any outside telephone lines at his lodge. Truman liked the ski club members and gave permission to install the telephone because he thought it would help his winter business. But Truman's interest in actually taking the ski club members on the three-mile trip up to their cabin in the Sno-Cat ran hot and cold.

"You know how Harry was," recalls club member Gunnar Nilsson, who had known Truman since 1929. "If he felt like taking you, he took you; if he didn't, then 'to hell with you.'" But Nilsson concocted a clever plan to ensure better service from Truman. He proposed to make Truman an honorary member of the club—complete with a big plaque with a gold stamp on it. The presentation was supposed to be a light-hearted, fun evening and ski club members were most surprised by Truman's reaction. "He cried when he got that thing," Nilsson says. "But from then on, Harry never refused us a ride."

One of Truman's other friends from the Longview Ski Club was George Bowers, a colorful used-car dealer who was one of the few people capable of trading four-letter barbs with Truman. George was one of the few who managed to take his boat up to Spirit Lake when he was staying in one of Truman's cabins. Truman always told George, "George, goddamnit, get that damn boat out of here; this is my dock." And George always told Truman, "Oh go to hell, Truman, you old son-of-a-bitch" and went ahead and used his boat anyway. "I didn't call him Harry and I didn't call him Truman," George recalls. "He'd see me coming and say 'How ya doin', my short-peckered little friend?' And I'd say 'Pretty good, you ugly old son-of-a-bitch.' That's the way it was with us."

George was one of the few people with whom Truman shared his secret of Big Foot. For years, there had been rumors that the hairy apelike creature, also known as a Sasquatch, inhabited the area. One of the canyons in the area was known as Ape Canyon, following a legendary encounter in 1924 between a group of miners and several of the creatures. A group of Boy Scouts were also supposed to have been attacked by the creatures several years later.

Truman relished Big Foot stories, especially since every report of the mysterious animals inevitably increased business at his lodge. Then one day he got the idea that he could probably help the Big Foot legend along a little. He meticulously carved a pair of big wooden feet and then fastened them securely to an old pair of shoes. At the first fresh snowfall, Truman took the Sno-Cat up the mountain and traipsed around in his homemade big feet where he was sure skiers would see the tracks.

The trick couldn't have worked better, Truman later told George: "When those skiers saw those giant footprints, they were sure Big Foot was around. Some of them ran off the mountain so fast you could have shot marbles on their coattails. I've never seen so much hell raised."

George's own favorite Truman story is set on a frigid spring morning at 6 A.M. One of the guests staying in a cabin couldn't get his gas heater going and was banging on Truman's front door trying to get help. But all the man heard from inside were the muffled sounds of a man and woman arguing. Finally Truman came to the door. He stood there with one hand over his mouth and the other holding a glass filled with frozen water and his false teeth; Eddie, still arguing, was right behind him in the same predicament. They had both placed their false teeth in glasses of water and set them on the windowsill when they went to bed. The cold had frozen them solid.

Truman didn't usually rent cabins when there was a lot of snow on the ground, but he had made an exception for this regular customer who stood shivering in the cold, wondering what to do as the arguing continued. Finally he insisted and the toothless Truman followed him down to the cabin, mumbling and grumbling that the heater had been working fine the day before. He turned on the heater and an explosion rocked the cabin. "It singed all my goddamn hair off and his, too, and it damn near blew the guy out the goddamn cabin door," Truman said later. "I thought the son-of-a-bitch was going to sue me."

Another of Truman's ski club friends was Alan Cripe, who had first gone to Spirit Lake in 1939. Cripe and his brother were particular favorites of Truman's because they always enjoyed singular fishing success at Spirit Lake. Their secret was using Migorino trout plugs as lures instead of bait. Cripe once pulled a huge trout from the lake that weighed 11 pounds. One summer's day, Truman loaned them some poles and rented them a boat. Both brothers quickly caught trout weighing about six pounds, then put them in the trunk of their car. Truman, sizing up an opportunity, intercepted them. "Well by God, you're not going to move your car until I round up the people in my cabins and show them there are some goddamn big fish in this lake," he said. "It's not going to cost you any money for the boat, the poles or anything; everything's on me, but don't go running away." Truman soon returned with all his guests in tow and showed them the fish; he was soon renting boats and fishing gear like crazy.

Alan Cripe had a falling-out with the mercurial Truman, as did many others over the years. Truman had accused Cripe of sinking one of his boats and Cripe angrily responded that he "could go to town and buy boats for $12 that were better than any of the boats you had." The two didn't talk for a year. But as usually happened, time soothed the anger and Truman flagged Cripe down one time when he was up at Spirit Lake. "Come on in here and have a drink," Truman told him. "Let's be friends again; we've been friends for too damn many years to become enemies. Besides, you're the best goddamn fisherman on the lake and I'm losing business because you're not fishing up here any more."

Truman and Eddie hosted semiannual parties for the Longview Ski Club. There was a party in the winter and a party in the summer. "It was a potluck and everybody would set their food out on the bar and Truman would throw that damn beer out there and we'd dance all night long," George Bowers remembers. "That's how I got to know Eddie. She loved to dance and we'd jitterbug until four in the morning. And Truman would grab my wife Lorraine or Rob Quoidbach's wife Mary Lou and say, 'Come on now, honey; let's dance. But don't pick up your feet, just shuffle.'" Truman would have the phonograph going loud, then he'd start up the nickelodeon. Or Eddie would play the 1882 player piano, which Truman gave her as a birthday present, and put on one of the 250 rolls of music and everybody would sing. The beer kept flowing, compliments of Truman, who was truly in his element.

Truman seldom seemed so cocksure of himself, so totally

in command, on the few occasions when Eddie's whole
family came to call on holidays. I remember spending the
Christmas of 1952 at the lodge with Mom, my two sisters and
Dayle's fiancé. I also remember spending the Christmas of
1954 there when all 10 of Eddie's relatives came to visit—the
only time that ever happened. The lodge was decorated
with hundreds of lights and it looked like a winter wonder-
land scene straight from a Christmas card with the lights
reflecting on the heavy snow and huge icicles. Auntie Eddie
was beaming. She went from relative to relative hugging us
and urging us to sample some of the special Christmas
goodies she'd spent weeks preparing. But amidst all the
festive merriment, Truman sat off by himself and was un-
characteristically quiet. He looked like a spoiled little boy
who was pouting because no one was paying him enough
attention. Truman relished being Auntie Eddie's one and
only star and he didn't like sharing her love and her
limelight with anyone.

8:

HE had bought two Cadillacs before, but Truman's pink 1956 Coupe de Ville was so special that he never bought another. It was a custom order, with just about every extra that the Golden Age of Detroit could provide: gold-colored wire wheels, a Continental kit for the spare, air conditioning, white leather upholstery, and an El Dorado engine with two four-barrel carburetors that provided all the power a life-long speeder like Truman could possibly want.

As he had done before, Truman decided to pick up the Cadillac himself at the factory in Detroit. It was to be a grand trip, a motor tour of much of the country, including his first visit to Washington, D.C., where he would get to see his good friend William O. Douglas. Eddie would of course come along, as would their good friends Art and Nadine Clarkson, the owners of the Oasis Tavern in Castle Rock, whom they had known since 1945. Truman first drove to Seattle to buy clothes. He was certainly not about to visit a Supreme Court Justice wearing chinos and a long-sleeved sport shirt. He bought a new suit, dress shirts, suspenders, ties, a topcoat, and a snazzy broad-brimmed hat. When he returned to Spirit Lake with his purchases, Eddie hardly recognized him.

The Trumans and the Clarksons were driven to Vancouver, British Columbia, by the grateful Centralia Cadillac salesman. They boarded the elegant Canadian Pacific train that would take them to Toronto, then caught another train to Detroit.

The night of their arrival in the Motor City, there was a bit of a problem and Truman was mostly to blame, as he would be several times on the trip. Art Clarkson had made an in-depth inspection tour of the five bars in their hotel and the two women had gotten "all gussied up" for their dinner date with an insurance executive, who was a friend of Truman. But Truman was sitting in bed sulking, as he sometimes did when he drank. Words of persuasion wouldn't budge him—he just didn't want to go to dinner. Art finally ordered four steaks from room service and Truman polished off his while still sitting in bed in his shiny silklike undershirt. Then the insurance executive arrived and Truman greeted him from bed with a hearty "Come on in!" They shared several cocktails and had a fine, fun time.

By the next evening, Truman was ready to see the town, and the foursome ate at a posh Detroit restaurant called Cliff Bell's. It was exactly the kind of place Truman liked when he went to the Big City—with waiters in tuxedos and a solicitous maître d' whom Truman could slip a bill, insuring his party the best table in the house. Truman was no wilderness bumpkin when he was on the road; he wanted everything first class—the atmosphere, the service, the food, the booze. That night at Cliff Bell's, Truman knocked down a dozen flaming Drambuies, flame and all.

Before leaving Seattle, Nadine Clarkson had warned him: "The first time you're drunk behind the wheel, I'm flying home." Truman assured her he wouldn't drink during the day when they were driving, and kept that promise. The nights, of course, were different.

Naturally, the highlight of the Detroit stop was the General Motors plant, and Truman's new pride and joy. The pink Cadillac was really a pastel; the extras and accessories exceeded his expectations; and the Continental kit, well,

Truman thought it was a truly beautiful automobile. He could hardly wait to give it a good run on the open road. From Detroit, Truman navigated a course to Niagara Falls, pushed the accelerator to the floor, and smiled at the surge of speed. Soon enough, he glanced in the rear-view mirror and saw the flashing red lights of a patrol car. He promptly pulled over.

The patrolman asked to see his license and was surprised at the name he saw: "Harry Truman, huh?" "Yep," replied Truman, "right from the hills of West Virginia and a damn good Democrat, too!"

The officer handed back Truman's license and simply said, "Take it a little easier, sir."

From Niagara Falls they drove to New York City, where they stayed three days. The next stop was Atlantic City, with its Boardwalk and its pigeons. While the birds kept their distance from everyone else, they swarmed around Truman, just as the birds at Spirit Lake always did when he fed them. Then it was on to Washington, the stop Truman had long been anticipating.

The Clarksons went off for dinner with friends and Truman and Eddie went to the University Club to meet Justice Douglas. His greeting was hearty and they had a couple drinks—reminiscing about their times together two summers before at Spirit Lake. Douglas told them about a conversation he'd had with his old poker-playing chum, Harry S. Truman. "There's a guy out there in Washington State with your same name," Douglas had told the former President, "who can outdrink you and probably outcuss you, too." But once the laughter had died from the story, Douglas excused himself and said he couldn't stay for dinner; he had to be in Philadelphia the next day for the Army-Navy game.

Truman was crestfallen. He had expected to spend the entire evening, and maybe longer, with his famous friend and he was deeply disappointed by Douglas's early exit. When he and Eddie returned to their hotel, Truman started drinking and refused to eat. It was only after the Clarksons returned that Truman was finally persuaded to go to dinner at a restaurant down the street from his hotel.

After three days of sightseeing in the capital, they were on the road again, heading south to Georgia and the town of Bainbridge, where friend Tom Franklin owned a 3,000-acre sugar plantation. Franklin was the owner of a motel in Las Vegas where Truman and Eddie often stayed. The visit in Bainbridge included an afternoon of quail-hunting for the men—with Tom at the wheel of his own new Cadillac, plowing right through the fields and sending cane flying every which way, while Truman sat in the back seat with three hunting dogs, mixing drinks. The quail escaped unscathed that day.

The foursome then headed for New Orleans. Truman and Eddie had been good friends and had often exchanged letters with Mary Cloney, ex-wife of the mayor of Longview, who had returned to her native New Orleans after her divorce. She had arranged a stay for the Trumans and the Clarksons that literally dripped with Southern hospitality.

On their second night in New Orleans, they were invited to a big party at the home of one of the city's leading citizens, a brewery executive. Several members of the New Orleans social scene were at the party. Truman was the center of attention, as usual. Then the subject of blacks and their treatment in the South came up. Truman told his host, in no uncertain terms, that he didn't approve of "this discrimination against colored people." It was 1955, only a year after the Supreme Court had ordered all schools desegregated in *Brown* v. *The Topeka Board of Education,* and an argument soon ensued between Truman and his host.

Truman got hotter by the minute. Art, Nadine, and Eddie all tried to calm him down, reminding him that this was no way to act as a guest in someone's home, and that politics had no place in a social evening. But Truman wouldn't listen. He said he was driving back to Washington State by himself that very night, stormed out of the house, started

up the Cadillac and sped off. He drove as far as their New
Orleans motel.

Truman might well have wanted to drive back to Washington that night, but there was a slight problem—he had no
money. At the start of the trip, it had been decided that the
men would carry half the money for the trip and the women
would carry the rest. But by New Orleans, both Truman's
and Art's wallets were empty and all the remaining money
was in Nadine's and Eddie's purses. So Truman's only choice
that night was to stop at the motel.

The other three returned at 5 A.M. Truman still wanted
to continue the argument with Eddie, but she headed instead to the Clarksons' adjoining room and convinced Art
to take her place in Truman's room. Only a few hours later,
the phone rang. It was their host from the night before.
"Come on over," he said cheerily, "the drinks are all fixed!"
So off they went again to his huge estate, Truman included,
acting as if nothing had happened the night before. He had
made his point and saw no need to resume the argument.

They were soon into the homestretch of their long cross-
country journey. They went to Las Vegas, then to Reno. But
it was on a day trip to Lake Tahoe that disaster struck. In the
late afternoon they were returning to their Reno motel
when a Cadillac coming toward them skidded into the
gravel on the shoulder and then spun directly into their
path. There was no time to stop and the other Cadillac
smashed broadside into Truman's. The impact of the crash
knocked Truman's false teeth right out of his mouth, and
Nadine would forever remember the image of him with his
false teeth in one hand and his head resting on the steering
wheel, moaning about how the whole front end of his prize
Cadillac was smashed in. They were all rushed to the hospital. Eddie had a broken leg. Art's leg was also badly hurt,
and a night at the hospital was recommended for them
both. But Art and Eddie vetoed that. "I told Harry, 'I don't
trust you with my wife,'" Art recalls, "and Eddie said she
didn't trust Harry with her, either." So everyone agreed to go

back to the motel, the Pony Express, where, as luck would have it, their rooms were on the second floor. "We had a helluva time getting upstairs," Art says.

The trip ended with two people on crutches and the four of them crammed into a rented Chevrolet along with 13 pieces of luggage. It took months of haggling until the insurance claims were finally settled and Eddie received $3,000 for her personal injury—most of which Truman used to build two more cabins at the resort.

While Truman and Eddie were gone, the lodge was looked after by Jim Lund, Chickaloon's son, and Peg-leg Al Brimsfield. Peg-leg was Truman's World War I buddy who periodically worked at the resort and was a gentle, comical character who found humor in his missing leg. In the summer he would frequently be seen swinging the hollow leg in the icy Toutle. "Come join me," he'd say, "I'm just coolin' my cocktails." Indeed, my sister Dayle once saw him pull a bottle out of the hollow leg.

Truman's two best friends were both named John—John "Chickaloon" Lund, the game warden, and John Garrity, a railroad executive from Minnesota. They were vastly different characters.

Lund was assigned to Spirit Lake and Mount St. Helens as game warden in 1947 and he was a serious-minded man with a selfless dedication to his work. He stayed as game warden until 1963 when he retired, although as his son Jim recalls, "He never quit. He was the game warden until the day he died." Lund had heard about Truman's legendary poaching exploits from other game wardens and was determined he was going to catch Harry Truman once and for all. The two adversaries couldn't help but become friends as they tested and teased each other for years.

During the war, Lund worked on the railroad in Alaska, where one of the lines ended at the village of Chickaloon, east of Anchorage. The nickname stuck throughout his life, although Truman called him Chick. Not long after he arrived at Spirit Lake, Lund and his son built a cabin near

Truman's cabin on Studebaker Creek. He positioned it there specifically so he could observe Truman's comings and goings. This bold move surprised Truman, who resolved to outwit the warden any way he could. He often baited Lund, frantically firing guns in the area at nothing in particular, or leaving articles of clothing as "clues" that led nowhere.

Stealing from each other was another game the two often played. "My dad and Harry Truman were the two finest cedar-shake thieves in the world," Jim Lund recalls. "You really had to keep an eye on those two old buggers." He remembers the time he and his father had spent long hours sawing by hand a large load of wood using a crosscut saw. They went to get a trailer to cart the wood away, but when they returned, the wood was gone. There was a note on a nearby stump: "Kilroy was here!" The Lunds had little doubt who Kilroy was.

Chickaloon Lund soon got his revenge. Reshaking the roofs at Truman's resort was a continuous job; as soon as one roof was finished, there was another one to do. Lund merely waited until Truman was about to reshake another roof, then scouted the woods to find a fine cedar tree sawed into shake-bolt lengths and carefully hidden by Truman. Those shakes did indeed end up on a roof—on Lund's cabin.

When the two weren't playing tricks on each other in the woods, they were often sharing coffee in the kitchen of the lodge. Eddie adored Chickaloon and she was also very fond of his son Jim, who is deaf. Chick's wife Margaret had somewhat different thoughts about Truman. She didn't care much for the way he always took advantage of her husband's generous good nature, and the way Truman monopolized his time. Chickaloon Lund spent countless hours working at Truman's resort, and the extra money he earned helped his family make ends meet. Lund did all the stonework around the lodge, building a brick fence with two large gateposts and lights on top. For all his efforts, he seldom got much acknowledgement from Truman, although Chickaloon was about the only person he and Eddie bought gifts for on their long trips—gifts like a large belt buckle with a 1921 silver dollar and a gallon jug from Mexico wrapped in sisal and filled with rum.

Jim Lund remembers the time he had driven all the way from Seattle to see his father on Father's Day. He found Chickaloon hard at work at Truman's. "Come on, Dad," Jim urged, "to hell with this." "No, Harry wants this done," his father replied.

"Harry worked Chickaloon from daylight in the morning," says Jim, "but Harry didn't know it was wrong. Truman was a mean, ornery, self-centered, savage old bastard. He was flat-out honest about what he was and he didn't give a damn what you thought about it. He drove himself just as hard as he drove everybody else and he thought everyone had to work that way. This world would be a helluva lot better off if there were a few more like him."

Chickaloon Lund obviously shared some of the same feelings. He had been sent to Spirit Lake to catch a poacher, but soon discovered that Truman was not out in the woods shooting animals and selling their meat or their horns for trophies, as outlaw poachers do. When Truman killed animals, it was for food—and even then he was impossible to catch.

Truman's other best friend was John Garrity of White Bear Lake, Minnesota, for years the executive assistant to the chairman of the board of the Northern Pacific Railway. Truman was happy to let people think he owned the 50 acres where his resort sat, but in fact, it belonged to the railroad, which leased it to him. The Northern Pacific also owned the summit of Mount St. Helens.

Garrity's first trip to Spirit Lake was in the fall of 1954 when he accompanied Dwight Edgell, another railroad executive. Edgell had promised Garrity, "I'm going to introduce you to a fellow named Harry Truman who can talk more and faster than anybody you ever met in your whole life. He can talk while he's sneezing, coughing, yawning or anything else." Truman lived up to advance billing. When Edgell and Garrity drove up to the lodge at dusk, Truman watched them warily out the window, then came bounding out. "Well I'll be goddamned if it isn't old Dwight Edgell," Truman said. "I thought you fellows might be a couple of health inspectors; the only sons-of-bitches that ever come up here this time of year are the inspectors."

Garrity and Truman were soon introduced and Garrity remembers shaking a hand that felt "like sandpaper." Their friendship grew fast. Although 23 years younger than Truman, Garrity was a hard-talking bachelor with the Irish charm of a leprechaun. "We just kind of jelled," Garrity recalls. "Harry was foolish for his age; I was foolish for mine." Garrity frequently took trips west for both business and pleasure, and always found a way to visit Spirit Lake and his friend Truman. Their reunions were always warm and often raucous. The bottles came out soon after the first bear-hug greeting on the front porch.

"The first night I'd get there, we'd rant until God knows what hour," Garrity remembers. "Then along about three or four o'clock in the morning, Eddie would come down and raise hell: 'Goddamn it, the both of you go to bed now!' She'd go back upstairs and Harry would whisper, 'Now we'll be real quiet and in 15 minutes she'll be back down to see what the hell we're doing.' And that's exactly what she'd do. Harry was a kid at heart."

Truman would tell Garrity some of his most sensitive thoughts about his love for Eddie, his friendship with Chickaloon, his often sad past and some of the hurts he'd suffered and hidden inside. Gradually Garrity came to see a far different Truman from what the public usually saw—a sentimental man who hid behind a mask of brusqueness and toughness, a thin-skinned man easily hurt by what others said about him, a man who often felt animals understood him better than people.

Truman trusted Garrity, and even told him his thoughts about the 1961 death of his only child, his daughter Betty.

She had been married to a logger in 1946 and they had had two children—the only grandchildren that Truman would ever have. She was divorced in 1959. Betty ended her life two years later, when she was just 39. Truman held himself responsible for what had happened, although Garrity was one of the very few people he told that. Joan Leonard, who had been best friends with Betty during their summers together working at the lake, remembers Truman's distraught actions at Betty's funeral: "It was sad—Harry didn't know how to express himself. He didn't want to cry; he wanted to be rough and rugged and strong. But it was obvious he blamed himself for Betty's death."

Not all of Garrity's and Truman's long talks took place late at night in the lodge. The two took several pack trips into the back country wilderness, sometimes accompanied by Chickaloon Lund. And Truman and Eddie would visit Garrity and friends back in Minnesota, traveling on the North Coast Limited. Truman often traveled in a private VIP car on the train and he usually got special treatment because of his high-placed friends in the railroad.

It was on one of these trips to Minnesota that Garrity introduced Truman to Dr. Roy Peterson, who also lived in White Bear Lake in the suburbs of St. Paul. Truman was soon calling him Doc, and Peterson became about the only doc Truman ever trusted or called his friend for the rest of his life. Truman wanted Doc to visit Spirit Lake and a back country pack trip was planned for the summer of 1961. But when the appointed time arrived, Peterson had to change his plans, and Garrity arrived at the lodge alone. Truman wouldn't stand for it. He put Garrity into the pickup and the two drove 25 miles down the highway to the nearest phone, at Kid Valley. Peterson was out of his office on an emergency, and Truman left a message with the doctor's answering service: "Tell that goddamned pill pusher that Harry Truman called." Finally Peterson changed his plans again and came for the visit.

They partied for two nights straight, and at one point in

the conversation Truman asked Doc, "Can you ride a
horse?" Peterson's cautious reply was that he considered
himself a "gentleman rider." Peterson was indeed a gentleman, so it was only natural that he thought he would be a
gentleman rider once he got on a horse. He didn't want to
admit that he had never ridden a horse in his life.

Early the next morning—after only a few hours of
sleep—the horses were all saddled up and Truman, Garrity,
Peterson, and Chickaloon Lund were ready to depart. A
small dispute arose over whether Peterson was going to take
his medical ditty bag into the back country. Truman told
him, "You'll be lucky if you just get yourself up there on the
horse. You're not going to be able to carry that damn ditty
bag." But Peterson was adamant. He took that ditty bag—a
doctor's satchel with two handles—wherever he went, he
said. So Peterson hooked the handles on the saddle horn,
stepped into the stirrup, and sat in the saddle—for at least a
second or so. The horse started bucking and Peterson went
flying, landing right on his rear end. Then the horse took
off and the ditty bag flew open and every time the horse
stopped to buck, medical paraphernalia and pills came
flying out.

In a scene worthy of the Keystone Cops, Truman and
Lund took off in hot pursuit of Peterson's horse, stopping to
scoop up spilled pills and needles and bandages along the
way. The horse headed for the campground, where two
ladies were sitting at a card table having a most civilized
breakfast of tea and crumpets. The horse blew right by
them, upsetting everything. Truman made sure they were
all right and asked one of the ladies, whose fancy hat was
now cocked over one eye, if she had seen a horse go
through. "No, I didn't see a horse," she calmly replied. "But
something just went through here."

Truman and Lund finally caught the horse and brought it
back to where Peterson was still sitting on the ground, just as
he had landed. He said he was okay and willing to give it a go
again, especially since the horse now seemed too tired to

care whether Doc was on his back or not. Truman couldn't resist the temptation to give his tenderfoot friends a trial by horseback. They rode and rode that first day and Truman wouldn't even stop to let them eat; drinking was all there was time for, he said, and Garrity got to feeling so tipsy that he almost fell off his horse. Finally at 10 P.M., they climbed down from the horses after 14 hours in the saddle. "If there had been any way of getting out of there without riding a horse the next day," Peterson recalls, "we certainly would have done it."

The next morning, however, Truman had them up early and back in the saddle again—riding higher and higher into the mountain country where the trails turned precariously narrow. Peterson remembers one stretch that was only 18 inches wide and a sheer drop straight down to one side. Peterson and Garrity both wanted to dismount and walk across, but Truman wouldn't let them.

The third night out, Truman became a camp casualty. He had gone to feed the horses and had taken out his knife to slash open a sack of oats. Instead, he slashed open a large gash in his own stomach. Luckily, Doc Peterson was along and stitched and bandaged Truman's stomach. Truman didn't want Eddie to find out, and swore everyone to secrecy. Eddie, of course, spotted the bandage soon after his return. "Truman," she said, "you'll do anything to get attention."

Years later, Truman went to Minneapolis for a hernia operation, which was to be performed by his favorite doc. Peterson gave his friend—then in his 70s—a thorough preoperative examination and found him in excellent shape. "He showed absolutely no ill effects from his drinking, but that was probably because Truman worked it off," Peterson says. "He was busy all the time; he was never still."

Truman's stamina amazed Peterson and the hospital staff. Within hours of the operation, he was standing up straight and walking around. Truman's recovery proceeded smoothly and Garrity decided it was time to smuggle in a bottle of Schenley's. Doc Peterson carried in the Coke. A party ensued and the three got louder and louder, but the members of the hospital staff were reluctant to intercede, since a doctor was part of the party. But Eddie wasn't so restrained. She unleashed a rare display of four-letter fireworks, calling them all "ornery S.O.B.'s" and accusing them all of acting like kids. She finally kicked Garrity and Doc Peterson out of Truman's room.

Two events—one good and one bad—would make 1962 a memorable year for Truman. Since the early 1930s, there had been talk and more talk about a new road that would go the three and a half miles from the turnaround at the Spirit Lake Campground up the steep climb to the timber line— the general route Truman had followed when pulling Longview Ski Club members behind his Sno-Cat. The road was finally dedicated on September 29 of 1962 in a pouring rainstorm. A crowd of 150 people watched as Congresswoman Julia Butler Hansen cut the ribbon. Truman, who had long supported the idea of the road and lobbied for its funding, stood proudly in the crowd.

Exactly two weeks after the dedication ceremony, the worst storm ever recorded in the Pacific Northwest ripped through the area. It would forever be known as the Columbus Day Storm. Hurricane-force winds of up to 170 miles per hour ravaged an area 125 miles wide and 1,000 miles long. The nightlong screaming storm caused the death of 48 people and paralyzed the region. Huge trees scored direct hits on parked cars and homes, statues toppled, and thousands of telephone poles snapped all the way from Northern California through Oregon and Washington and into British Columbia.

The full force of the storm socked Spirit Lake and Truman's resort. For years afterwards, Eddie would recall the horror of that night as she and Truman sought refuge in the basement. The damage at the resort was extensive—nine cabins were smashed and the boat dock broke away from its mooring. The Spirit Lake Highway was so littered with fallen trees that the Trumans were stranded for two weeks.

But the saddest effect of the storm was on the old-growth firs that had surrounded the lodge and the cabins. Some were 250 feet tall and hundreds of years old, and many had been blown down. Tall trees which have grown used to the shelter of numbers cannot stay standing long when many of their neighbors are gone. The survivors posed a direct threat to the resort, and all of them had to be cut down.

Truman had gone out in 1952 and paid $3,500 for a new D-2 Caterpillar Cat, a small bulldozer with tracks. After the awful Columbus Day Storm, he used the Cat to push the stumps and unsalvagable timber into huge piles behind the lodge. Truman's repeated requests for Forest Service permission to burn the piles were turned down because of the fire danger, and the piles—which were almost as tall as the lodge itself—scarred the scenery for years. One afternoon a friendly off-duty ranger stopped by at Truman's cocktail hour. While Truman coasted with Coke, he fixed a couple of "Harry Truman specials" for the ranger. As usual Truman had something in mind. He again asked for permission to burn the stump piles and the ranger blithely granted it. Truman seized the moment and rushed out to the boat-house, where he grabbed as many gallons of gas as he could carry. He climbed up the pile, poured gas all over it, jumped clear and flipped a match. The wood quickly became a raging inferno. The ranger, by now nervous and very sober, rushed up to the Forest Service work center, returning with a fire engine and a crew of men. They nervously strung fire hoses everywhere and then watched Truman circle the fire as if some sort of celebration were taking place. "Now look at that, boy, ain't that beeauuuuuti-ful?" he crowed. "Boy, that does my heart good."

Truman loved the D-2 Cat, even during tree removal. After his beloved pink Cadillac, it was probably his favorite toy, and he steadfastly refused to sell it. Truman sometimes told friends, "When I die, I'm going to take my D-2 Cat with me to heaven. If I can't take it with me, I'm not going!" Truman kept the Cat in perfect mechanical condition, slick and clean and ready to work. He did the same thing with the many mechanical things he accumulated at Spirit Lake over the years—enough to stock a general hardware store. A partial list of the items would include:

A 1956 Cadillac Coupe de Ville
A 1967 Chevrolet pickup truck
A D-2 Caterpillar Cat
A Sno-Cat
A Johnson snowmobile
A Yamaha 55 and a Yamaha 80 motorcycle
A Vespa 150 motor scooter
A Cushman motor scooter
Seven chainsaws, including an 11-horsepower Diston
A snow blower
Three power lawnmowers
One hundred boats
Eight canoes
A Century motor launch and a Chris Craft launch
Movie projectors and 8mm and 16mm movie cameras
Nine TV sets
An 1886 player piano with 250 rolls of music
Assorted stereo equipment
Two pinball machines
An arsenal of guns—most accumulated during Pro-
    hibition—which included a .410 shotgun pistol, a
    .22 Colt pistol, a .22 rifle, a 16-gauge shotgun, a
    .30-.06 rifle, a .30-.30 Winchester, a .300 Savage with
    an octagon barrel, a .22 Smith and Wesson pistol,
    and the .45 caliber Thompson machine gun.

Truman kept most of his guns well hidden, but one day he took the machine gun from its hiding place and brought it down to the boathouse. Jim Lund remembers that he, Red Hiles, and Truman shot at a ten-inch-thick fir tree until it toppled over.

The 1960s were mostly a happy time for Truman. Business was good, with many repeat customers and friends returning to Mount St. Helens Lodge. Relations with relatives continued to be mostly on Truman's own terms, which is what he preferred. The steady stream of Eddie's nieces who had worked summers at Spirit Lake dwindled as we graduated from high school and found full-time employment.

When the five of us nieces grew up and got married, we all had the ceremonies in the off season in hopes that Auntie Eddie and Truman would attend. But we were all disappointed: they never made it to any of the weddings. It was just one of the family disappointments we had come to expect, largely the result, we felt, of Truman's distaste for family obligations and having to share Eddie with anybody. Perhaps the saddest example of that was the many times Truman and Eddie would visit friends or relatives in Seattle, but would usually avoid visiting Tekla Natalia Lund— Eddie's mother—who lived downtown, not far from the Olympic Hotel, where the Trumans usually stayed. The other relatives they visited were always sworn to secrecy and were warned not to tell Grandma about the Seattle visits. Gram always got excited when she received one of Eddie's newsy letters, and never complained about how seldom she saw Eddie and Truman. But the whole situation always made me feel very uneasy.

I was married to Lee Rosen in 1956 and we had three children—Keith in 1958, Teresa in 1960, and Chris in 1965. After I started having children, we usually saw Truman and Auntie Eddie only once or twice a year. He just did not like having little children around, no matter whose they were. He had posted two *No Minors* signs between the front doors of the lodge years before, and the signs had only partially to do with the serving of alcoholic beverages. He would not permit families with little children to stay in the lodge. He didn't want his peace and quiet disturbed, he said.

As our children grew up, we spent vacations at Spirit Lake. Sometimes we'd rent a cabin at Truman's, but often to

save money we'd camp. I was embarrassed to tell Truman
the first time we camped, knowing how he felt about campers. But he and Auntie Eddie came over to the campground
to visit us that night and we shared hot toddies around the
campfire. Truman couldn't resist rummaging through our
camping gear and passing judgement. "Well," he said, "if
you've joined the goddamn squatters, at least I'm glad to see
you got some decent gear."

During one of the summers when we did rent a cabin,
Truman pulled another of his playful tricks on us. He came
down to the cabin when Lee and I were gone and enlisted
the help of our sons Keith and Chris. Keith emptied the
trash can and Truman smeared honey all over the lid. "Now
don't you tell your folks about this," he said. "We're going to
have a little fun with the bears tonight." At about 4 A.M., we
all awoke to the loud sound of a bear turning over the trash
can. Keith ran for the flashlight and we all watched as the
bear took long licks on the lid's surface, then lost control of it
and had to chase it as it rolled down to the beach. Truman
poked his head in the cabin early. "How'd you kids sleep last
night?" We all laughed at his joke, and so did he.

Relations with his relatives were not always that cheery.
Truman's relationship with his sister Geri Whiting was
sometimes stormy. He had decided to add a new restaurant
and lounge 100 yards from the lodge on the banks of the
North Toutle River. He enlisted the assistance of Buck Whiting and several other men, and they built it in the spring of
1958. The restaurant was modern and well equipped, and
the Star Light Room cocktail lounge was a perfect place to
sip a drink and watch the mountain. There was a complete
apartment in the basement. Truman leased the restaurant
to the Whitings for several years, but it was a losing proposi-
tion and they closed it forever in 1967 when Truman and the
Whitings had a parting of ways.

Truman had other problems, some with the Washington
State Department of Revenue. In 1964, a ruling had been
passed requiring that sales tax no longer be collected on

rental property. Truman didn't trust the ruling or the tax men and he continued to collect sales tax on his rental boats and equipment. One day an employee of the Vancouver, Washington, tax office rented a boat at Spirit Lake and then refused to pay the sales tax. He told Truman he shouldn't be charging it. Truman's response to that was simple and straightforward—he pushed the man into the lake.

The sales tax controversy simmered for some time and the state reversed its directive in 1966. Now, Truman was going to be required to pay two years of sales tax he had been instructed not to collect. The Vancouver tax man wanted nothing to do with another encounter with Truman; he asked Lloyd Sverdrup, Truman's accountant from Longview, to tell him about the change.

Sverdrup went up to the lodge, found Truman in bed with a cold and told him the bad news. "He went clear through the roof," Lloyd remembers. "There was nobody in that bed for five minutes. I just sat there while Truman went through his tirade and I let him unwind himself. When he finally shut up, I said, 'Well what else have you got to say?' And Truman replied, 'I'm not going to say a damn thing; I guess we'll just pay it.' Harry had three languages going: the American English, the Swearing, and the Bullshit; and when those three got mixed together, you had to be able to analyze what you were listening to."

Another constant concern for Truman was his property lease with the railroad. The Northern Pacific Railroad and the Burlington Northern Railroad—its successor—kept Truman on three-year leases for years. This irked Truman; his investment on the 50 acres rose to nearly $1 million and he often complained to Eddie about the railroad. She would say he was small potatoes to the big railroad and he would always reply, "I might be the smallest licensee, but—god-damned—I'm the loudest!" Truman's worries grew as the railroad proceeded to sell off just about all the land it owned in the area except the summit of Mount St. Helens and the land under Truman's resort.

Truman's good friend John Garrity went to bat for him. He brought his boss Ed Stanton, the railroad's executive vice-president, out to meet Truman at Spirit Lake in 1966. He and Truman got along well, but Truman kept bellowing about his short-term leases. Stanton listened patiently and finally said, "Tell you what I'm going to do, Truman. I'm going to give you a 20-year lease. To do more than that, I'd have to go to the board of directors and they would think I'm nuts to give you a lease longer than that. You're 70 years old already."

Truman started to scream and holler. "Goddamn it, Ed, I'm going to outlive you and that sanctimonious George Pohl [general manager of the railroad properties]. Hell, all of these railroad fellows are dying and I'm going to outlive all of you. I need a lease that's going to take me up to when I'm 125 years old." But secretly, Truman was "tickled to death" with the 20-year lease, as he told Garrity later. He just couldn't let one of the railroad bigwigs know how pleased he was. The lease made certain that his beloved land and his resort at Spirit Lake would stay secure until 1986, when he would be 90.

Later, Garrity came up with the idea that Truman should receive some sort of recognition for the 40 years he had devoted to his oasis on the railroad's land. It would require the okay of C.R. "Bob" Binger, who had just joined the railroad as president of the resource division. Garrity was uncertain whether Binger would approve—he didn't know him very well, but what he did know was that Binger was a "very strict fellow" who didn't swear or even drink coffee, a man with a reputation of being all business.

Garrity invited Binger to visit Truman's resort with considerable trepidation. Binger was indeed far different from Truman, but he enjoyed his stay at the resort—including his climb of Mount St. Helens with Rob Quoidbach. Binger told Garrity to proceed with his plans.

Garrity wrote a special inscription to be placed on a bronze plaque along with an etched likeness of Harry Tru-

man and Mount St. Helens. Then he enlisted the help of
Chickaloon Lund who would build a brick monument for
the plaque. The ceremony was all set for a Saturday night.
Eddie hired a cook so she could enjoy it herself, and she
invited the guests who would take over the entire resort.
The guest list included railroad executives like Binger and
Stanton; Forest Service friends like Ross Williams, forest
supervisor of the Gifford Pinchot National Forest, Jim
Langdon, and Chuck Tonn; Longview Ski Club friends like
the Quoidbachs, the Nilssons, the Wests, and the Cripes;
and Truman's best personal friends like Doc Peterson, John
Garrity, and Chickaloon Lund. No one from the family was
invited to attend. Truman had no idea about the plaque or
the big binder full of congratulatory letters that Garrity had
solicited. He just expected a big anniversary celebration.
There was a roped-off area around the brick monument,
and Truman kept hopping behind the rope, hoping to get
to make a speech. But Garrity kept telling him, "Goddamn
it, Harry, get the hell out of here; we're not ready for you
yet."

At dusk, they all went outside and gathered around the
monument. Several people gave speeches, and some told
anecdotes about Truman. Then Bob Binger stepped forward, made a short speech and presented the bronze plaque
to Truman. His eyes filled with tears as he read the inscription penned by Garrity:

> This recreation development on the south shore of
> Spirit Lake was pioneered by Harry R. Truman. He
> came here in 1928 [actually, 1926] from Castle Rock
> over a logging road and made the last few miles on
> snowshoes. He built a home here in 1929 and erected
> tent frames which he rented to campers and fisher-
> men. In 1937, sparks from a fireplace ignited a
> bearskin rug and completely destroyed his home. He
> built the present main lodge in 1939. Severe wind-
> storms destroyed most of the cabins in 1950 and again

in 1962, but he persevered despite the elements and hardships and rebuilt his camp after each disaster.

It is in recognition of this rugged, salty, pioneering spirit that the Northern Pacific Railway respectfully dedicates this plaque to Harry R. Truman, in September of 1969.

Then Garrity stepped forward. He told a few quick stories about Truman and what they had meant to him. Then he said there were many other people who had similar thoughts and a few of them had put those thoughts into words in this binder — which Truman would later come to call his Bible. There were few things Truman was ever as proud of, few things he ever wanted to share so with friends and family in later years. He always handed the binder over, saying, "Look at this goddamn Bible I got from my company. Just read those letters, read 'em aloud. That'll tell you what they think of ol' Truman."

When Garrity finished his speech, Truman stepped forward with his eyes still moist from the plaque presentation. But he really started to bawl when he opened the binder and read some of the letters:

MAN OR MOUNTAIN

Aloof and warm
Stoic and friendly
Simple and complex
Persistent in spite of obstacles
And, above all, always interesting,
With Eddie always near.
A description of:
Harry Truman
or
Mount St. Helens
And, who can tell the difference?
K.P. Tomlinson
Skeets Tomlinson

A salute to Harry Truman

Harry, on this auspicious occasion of Northern Pacific's recognition of your more than 40 years at the lake, Karole joins me in extending our congratulations and best wishes to you and Eddie—and may you require several more extensions of your lease.

Roy L. Peterson, M.D.

Dear Harry,

Your forty years at Spirit Lake has probably revised the entire folklore and body of legends of that historic area. The strawberries and the bears have also grown bigger and bigger, thanks to you.

I hope you have got those hot stoves under better control and that they have stopped moving around to your annoyance.

Harry, make the next forty years the same as the first forty. But do be careful; and remember that I am not always there to take care of you.

Yours faithfully,
William O. Douglas

9:

TRUMAN never feared death for himself. He had had such a long and richly rewarding life that thoughts of his death did not particularly disturb him, nor did they take up much of his time. Death would probably come, as did so many of the events in his life, with all the suddenness and unpredictability of winter weather on Spirit Lake. And since Truman was 13 years older than Eddie, he had made reasonable plans for the probability that he would die before she did, and he would take his place next to his daughter Betty in the Mountain View Cemetery in Centralia. (Both his mother and father were also buried there.) Then the railroad would find someone else to take over the lease and Eddie would move down to their mobile home overlooking the Columbia River at Prindle, about 110 miles from Spirit Lake, where she could live the rest of her life surrounded by the flowers she loved and the telephone and all the electric appliances she couldn't have up at the lodge. She could join Truman and Betty later.

But in the first week of September, 1975, all those well-made plans would dissolve and Truman would become a lonely and tormented soul. There were two deaths in two days that week at Mount St. Helens Lodge and things would never come close to being the same there again.

Labor Day weekend ended on Monday, September 1, and another summer's hectic rush was finally over. Truman was 79 and Eddie was 66, and handling the hundreds of summer visitors had become more and more difficult. Now they were looking forward to the fall days with time to relax and time for themselves — when they'd stroll through the woods side by side, picking vine-maple branches ablaze with bright colors and bringing them back to the lodge for decoration.

There was unusual excitement that next Saturday, September 6. Truman and Tim Hambleton, who had worked at the resort that summer, were putting away the boats for the winter. A small plane circled the lake in some sort of trouble and Truman watched warily as it lost altitude. "That goddamned son-of-a-bitch is gonna hit my lodge," yelled Truman as he and Tim ran from the boat dock following the plane's path.

But the plane, which had run out of gas on its way from Yakima to Longview, missed the lodge and landed on the Spirit Lake Highway, skidding across the road onto Truman's property. The pilot had no more of an injury than a scratch on his nose. But Truman acted as if one of the nation's major air disasters had just occurred. He raced off in his pickup to tell Rick Lawton of the Forest Service about the crash, then raced back to position himself to direct traffic around the downed plane, even though there was practically no traffic that time of year and the plane was so plainly visible that no one could possibly avoid seeing it.

Eddie wasn't feeling well that evening and went to bed early. Truman fixed Tim's dinner. Tim's parents were to pick him up the next day — Sunday, September 7 — and he had given them explicit instructions to bring a bottle of Schenley's for Truman and "the prettiest plant you can find for his wife." They arrived shortly after noon and Truman was moved by the thoughtfulness of the gifts. "Oh, Tim," he said, "Eddie's going to love this. She's not feeling good."

Truman took the plant up to her room and they both smiled and he told her to get some more rest while he went and visited their friends Rollie and Betty Mietzke. The Mietzkes, formerly proprietors of the Harmony Falls Lodge across Spirit Lake, had retired the year before and they were staying in their Airstream trailer over at the campground. Truman assured Eddie he'd be back soon.

What happened next would be etched forever in Tim's memory: "Harry came back to see how Eddie was and I remember he pulled in and went inside the lodge and a couple minutes later he came running back outside, got in the truck and raced back to the campground. It was about 3:30 or 4 in the afternoon, and Rollie rushed back down and about two minutes after they pulled up, the Forest Service truck pulled up and then the Berrys—who were running the Harmony Falls Lodge—came racing over in their boat."

Lawton of the Forest Service long remembers the sight of the then-frantic Truman when he came to fetch him in the bunkhouse of the work center. "He was saying, 'Eddie's sick! Eddie's sick!'" Lawton recalls. "He wasn't making any sense, other than that she was ill. He was in a frenzy; I'd never seen him like that. He wasn't in tears, but he was like somebody who was on the verge of tears. I couldn't make out what the problem was." Lawton grabbed the first aid kit from the wall of the bunkhouse and followed Truman back to the lodge. But the first aid kit was of no use. "By the time I got there, Eddie was lying on the bed and she was just as white as a sheet—and cold; there was no pulse," Lawton says. "There wasn't anything that I could do at that point, except try to calm Harry down."

Efforts to revive Eddie were futile and Lawton now believes Eddie had suffered a heart attack and that she was probably dead when Truman came to fetch him at the bunkhouse. It was as if Truman just couldn't accept that she was dead, and by saying that she was sick he could somehow undo what had happened.

Sadness settled over Spirit Lake late that Sunday afternoon. Rollie and Betty Mietzke moved their trailer to the

front of the lodge so they could be near Truman. Tim went
to tell the few guests that they were closing down. Truman
simply told people, "You don't have to pay me or anything."
Relatives were contacted.

Truman's grandson Barry Burnett was the first relative to
arrive at the lake. He and Truman went to Castle Rock
Monday morning to make the funeral arrangements. The
Mietzkes fixed breakfast and lunch for Tim and he handled
the boat business while they watched things at the lodge.
Later in the afternoon, Tim watched as Betty Mietzke
walked to their trailer and then emerged a couple minutes
later carrying two drinks back into the lodge. Suddenly, he
heard her screaming his name and he ran to the lodge.
"What's the matter?" he asked. "Rollie's had a heart attack!"
she cried.

He was lying on the floor of the main room of the lodge
and his wife was trying frantically to revive him using
mouth-to-mouth resuscitation. But it was having no effect
and she pleaded with Tim to go find help. He ran off, but by
the time he returned, Rollie Mietzke was dead. All the
15-year-old could do was cover him with a sheet.

Dusk had started to fall and Tim had gone to start the
generator when Truman and Barry returned from the funeral home. Tim remembers that moment: "All I wanted to
do was have a nervous breakdown and then Truman came
up to me and said, 'How's it going, kid?' Then I did two
things at once—I started crying and told Truman that
Rollie Mietzke was dead. Truman said, 'What! He can't be!'
and ran off to the lodge." Tim followed. When he got inside,
both Betty Mietzke and Truman were crying and Barry was
shaking his head and saying, "Oh no, oh no...." Soon
everyone was crying. None of them could believe that this
had happened exactly 24 hours after Eddie died.

We arrived shortly afterward. Mom had been called early
Monday morning and told about Eddie's passing and we
had headed off from Seattle to Spirit Lake, along with my
cousin Kathy. I remember seeing the hearse pulled up in

front of the lodge in the foggy evening—a ghostly vision—and I remember remarking that it seemed awfully late for them to be picking up Auntie Eddie. We would soon find out that the hearse was making its second visit to the lodge that day.

We walked in and were greeted by Truman and Betty Mietzke and their eyes were red and swollen. He gave Mom a hug and patted her awkwardly as she started to cry, then he proceeded to tell us what had happened only hours before we arrived.

Truman asked Kathy and me to try to find the boathouse cash box. He knew he had hidden it somewhere but his mind just couldn't remember where. So we searched and searched, finding piles of money in all the funny little places Truman always hid it—in drawers, in containers, under the linen in a cupboard under the back bar. It was like an Easter egg hunt. But we couldn't find the cash box and we told Truman we had looked everywhere except the pantry, which immediately rang a bell in his mind. He jumped up and scurried across the room to the pantry—which always reminded me of Fibber McGee's closet, only twice as large. He reached behind a pile of pots and pans which clattered to the wood floor and there was the cash box, amid the sprouting potatoes, the limp carrots, and the old onions. He was greatly relieved.

Truman fixed drinks for those who wanted them and some of us did. He and Betty were alternating between crying and laughing and I remember him trying to comfort her by saying, "Don't worry about it, Betty, now you're in the same damn boat that I'm in."

But the next morning was different as the impact of the deaths started settling in. Truman sat in the kitchen in his chair and I remember thinking that this man who had always seemed so young and full of vitality now looked every one of his 79 years. Truman was rocking back and forth in his chair, slowly moaning and wailing with his arms hugging his torso. It was as if wrapping his arms around himself would somehow keep his body from breaking apart. I wanted to put my arms around him, but I knew he wouldn't want that.

I had only seen Truman cry once before in my life and that was when we went up to the lake after his daughter Betty died. But then he cried and wiped his eyes and Auntie Eddie comforted him. This time he was without her and everyone around was crying, too. Truman asked Mom and me to find some clothes for Auntie Eddie to wear in the casket—he wanted to take them down to the funeral home that afternoon. Mom was still crying and I felt most uncomfortable searching through Auntie Eddie's things. We couldn't find any of her good clothes which, it turned out, were down at the home at Prindle. We finally found a nice brown-and-white blouse and a skirt that didn't quite match and a pair of pearl earrings. Then Mom took off the long double strand of pearls she was wearing so Auntie Eddie could wear that, too.

Truman and Barry went to town and stopped by the funeral home, then went from bank to bank in Castle Rock, Chehalis, and Washougal. Fearful of an impending visit from his unwelcome tax men following Eddie's death, Truman went to the vault at each bank, opened up safe deposit boxes he had rented, and stuffed all the cash into his pockets. Then he'd return to the pickup and transfer the cash to an attaché case, which by then was filled almost to overflowing. Although he was extremely distraught that afternoon, Truman hadn't lost his sense of humor entirely. In one of the boxes, he put a note that said, "April Fool, IRS."

That night, Barry built a big fire in the fireplace and Kathy and I sat by the fire with him. Mom went to bed early. Truman joined us after a while. He didn't say anything, he just looked into the flickering flames and his eyes filled with tears again. I remember Barry, a handsome, strapping young man of 24, went over and put his arm around Truman's shoulder and said ever so gently, "It'll be all right,

Grandpa." Eventually Truman went to bed and we could hear him sobbing throughout the night.

When we got up that Thursday morning, Truman was already dressed in a Pendleton outfit, ready to go to the funeral home. He took the pickup and stopped along the way—cutting branches of the bright vine maple Eddie and he always used to decorate the lodge in the fall.

Auntie Eddie loved flowers and I had never been to a funeral where there were so many. The funeral parlor was ablaze with bright colors from all the bouquets and wreaths and the branches Truman had brought. The casket lay on a bed of maple boughs, their crimson leaves next to the gray coffin. I remember Truman saying, "Just look at all those flowers. Everyone loved Eddie." The whole family was there, except my sister Elaine, who couldn't make it from her home in Alaska, and Grandma, whose health was failing so badly that we didn't dare tell her her daughter had died. There were so many people that the funeral parlor couldn't hold them all and I remember scanning the crowd and being surprised to see the face of Betty Mietzke, who had been especially kind to come when she had her own husband's funeral to attend.

After the burial in Centralia, we all drove to the home of Buck and Geri Whiting. Our side of the family hadn't socialized much with Truman's sister and her husband, and I had met them only a few times. But they had arranged a lovely buffet and it was something everyone appreciated. Truman, however, was most uncomfortable and impatient and soon asked Kathy to drive him back to the lake. He didn't say a word on the long trip back.

Truman wanted some company the next few days and it was decided that I would stay, along with my cousins Kathy and Carolyn. Mom was very upset and went back to Seattle with my husband Lee. I remember riding up the Spirit Lake Highway that afternoon and rounding the familiar bend as the lodge loomed up in front of us. Carolyn stopped the car and stayed frozen to the wheel. I felt the same way. It was

difficult to walk into the lodge knowing that Auntie Eddie
would never be there to greet us again.

Truman himself was having a most difficult time. He was
running in and out of the lodge, lost and disoriented. One
minute, he'd say, "Let's close the goddamned place down"
and the next minute, "No, we'll keep it open; that's what
Eddie would want." He finally decided to keep two cabins
open for the fall. Kathy and I cleaned the others for the
final time of the season. We folded the bedding and stacked
everything on the porches and Truman came by and loaded
it all in his pickup. We hopped on the tailgate and I felt like
16 again, working at the lake as the sunlight filtered through
the trees and its reflections sparkled on the rippling surface
of Spirit Lake.

The truck stopped and ended my reverie on the warm
autumn afternoon. Truman held the restaurant door open
as Kathy and I—hidden behind the huge piles of precariously carried blankets—walked in to set them on the tables
in the restaurant for storage. I had taken too big a load and
it tumbled to the floor. Truman started to cry uncontrollably
again. "Eddie was always doing that," he sobbed.

A neighbor from across the lake stopped by with something to eat and told Truman that she would be back Sunday
to help him with the thank-you notes. Carolyn and Kathy
tried to help him balance his books, and I worked in the
kitchen trying to clear away some of the clutter. I found
Auntie Eddie's engagement ring there in an ashtray filled
with needles and pins, buttons and paper clips. I remembered how proud she had been when Truman gave it to her
and how she liked to show off the small diamond with the
cherub on each side holding a tiny ruby. Auntie Eddie's
years of hard work had worn the cherubs flat. I gingerly
picked the ring out of the ashtray and took it over to Truman and handed it to him: "Truman, you may want to put
this someplace for safe keeping."

"No, you take it, kid," he said.

"I couldn't do that, I just don't want to see it get lost."

Truman made a motion waving me away with the back of his hand and said emphatically, "I want you to have it. You take it right now and I don't want to hear any more about it!" I was both moved and stunned.

After we left, Truman later made arrangements for Cy and Ruth Jacques of Toledo to stay with him that winter and take over the apartment below the restaurant. A few days before they were scheduled to move in, I drove down to Spirit Lake with my sister Elaine, who had flown down from Alaska. Truman seemed genuinely pleased to see us. Yet at the same time, I had an uncomfortable, almost eerie feeling. Everything was still exactly the way Auntie Eddie had left it. Since Truman had never given any thought to what would happen if Eddie died before he did, he seemed immobilized by her passing. He kept saying, "Why didn't God take me? Why did he take Eddie? Why?" He pored over the cards and letters of sympathy he'd received, showing them all to Elaine and me. And the man I had so seldom seen cry couldn't seem to quit.

That afternoon he said, "Come on, Shirley, I want to show you something." He buried his big, rough hands deep into a large plastic container of birdseed and corn that he kept on the back porch and filled his pockets and a pie tin. Then he walked down the back steps and started a high-pitched squawking: "Oh birds! Oh birds! Come on birds!" Then he whistled and alternated that with his bird calls. I looked out toward the lake and suddenly there were swarms of birds swooping down all the way across from Bear Creek. I watched spellbound as the birds circled and landed on Truman and the nearby bird feeders. They landed on his shoulders and on the bill of his baseball cap and Truman laughed his deep hearty laugh—the first time I'd heard him laugh like that since Auntie Eddie's death. Truman kept talking all the time and a little chickadee perched dead center on the top of his cap. The birds were fluttering and warbling overhead as Truman fed them and said, "You know in the winter they worry they won't get enough food, but I just go out and talk to them and tell them everything will be all right. Ol' Truman will take care of them."

The animals came to mean far more to Truman after Auntie Eddie's death. Boy had died in the early 1960s, and Truman hadn't wanted a dog to replace him, but there were 16 cats—some direct descendants of Gilbert—and a family of six raccoons lived under the back porch. Sometimes the cats and the raccoons would eat together in the kitchen, and sometimes Truman would feed raccoons out of his hands off the back porch, their little masked faces looking up at him expectantly. He bought far more food for the animals than for himself. Truman would tell his best friend John Garrity, "Hell, if it wasn't for the cats and raccoons and birds, I'd die of loneliness."

He was always willing to help other little animal friends he encountered around Spirit Lake. One time he was out walking and came upon a little beaver which had just chopped down a small tree and was having a heck of a time trying to drag it down to the water. Truman picked up one end and the beaver picked up the other and the two of them together finished the job.

His animal friends helped ease the ache of loneliness Truman felt after Eddie died, but everyone who knew them well saw a devastated man. "He dearly loved her," says Garrity. "When she died, it just destroyed him." Margaret Sverdrup, wife of Truman's accountant, remembers: "He'd start crying when he talked about her and shed buckets of tears. He quit caring about what happened to him after she was gone." Says Jim Lund: "After Eddie passed away, it was just like it blowed the wind out of that old bugger's sails. If he wasn't so damn tough, it would have killed him right away. But the old bugger was tougher than a boiled owl."

Truman's life at the lake seemed to proceed at half-speed. Things that had always been done faithfully around the resort before, were done infrequently if they were done at all. Painting and roofing and the constant chores all suffered. So did Truman's own appearance. His clothes were never as clean and well kept and he was never as well groomed after Eddie died. He lost weight and seemed to drink more, too.

In the depths of his loneliness, Truman continued to keep many things the way they were when Eddie died. He had a full bar filled with liquor in his restaurant but he steadfastly refused to pour any of it for anyone. "You'd go down there and he'd buy you a beer, but he would never pour you a drink out of one of those bottles," friend Dave Smith recalls. "The liquor that was there when Eddie died was something sacred to him because he and she would go down to that bar and have a drink together."

Truman felt the same way about his 1967 Chevy pickup truck and his 1956 pink Cadillac, which sat in his garage untouched for years. He had offers to buy the car, but he always declined them because he and Eddie had taken so many memorable trips in that car together.

But nothing showed Truman's dogged devotion to Eddie and her memory more graphically—and more poignantly—than their home at Prindle overlooking the Columbia River. And no place was more painful for Truman to visit, although he made it a point to go there, just as he made it a point to put flowers or maple leaves on Eddie's grave in Centralia.

Tim Hambleton, who worked year-round for Truman after Eddie died, frequently went on the trips to Prindle and remembers: "Every time I went down there Truman gave me the grand tour. He'd take me all around and he'd point out the things she made and crocheted and he'd say, 'Eddie did all this stuff by herself; she'd just have a grand old time down here.'"

Truman had been willed the two and a half acres in Prindle and a tiny trailer by an old friend he'd slip $100 or $200 to every now and then. When Truman and Eddie first went there in the late 1960s, the property was a terraced mass of blackberry vines and underbrush. They spent hundreds of hours clearing it away and improving the place, which they came to call Tanglewood Terrace.

A large mobile home was bought and Truman had it put in front of the small trailer, which he converted to a greenhouse for Eddie. He covered both with matching siding. Eddie surrounded Tanglewood Terrace—or Eddie's dollhouse, as Truman sometimes called it—with flower gardens and fruit and magnolia trees that all flourished under her careful attention. Inside she had every modern appliance—a toaster, a mixer, a washing machine, a dishwasher—all things the lodge's inadequate generator couldn't handle.

"Truman left the place exactly like it was when she died," Tim says. "He never changed anything around. The picture of Eddie's mother's home in Sweden was still hanging over her bed, the handmade afghan was folded and placed where she had put it at the foot of the bed. All her good things were still hanging in the closet, like they were still waiting for her. Every time we went down to Prindle, Truman would take down boxes of things from the lodge. I think he was possibly thinking of moving there someday, although he always cried when he went there."

Truman's life at Mount St. Helens Lodge—half-hearted as it was—did go on. He continued to rent cabins and boats and sell beer by the bottle. He continued to have many repeat customers, people who had grown accustomed to his willingness to do just about anything he could for the people who kept coming back to his resort. But the summer of 1976 was Truman's first while trying to run the resort without a woman around, and it showed. Guests were particularly surprised to have to make their own beds.

The boat boys and staff that summer were Tim Hambleton and Stephen Gorringe, the son of my sister Dayle, and they can still recount loving horror stories about Truman's culinary attempts. "Truman was the lousiest cook I have ever been exposed to," Steve recalls. "His food was absolutely unbelievable. But I didn't want to say anything because it gave him a certain amount of pride; I can cook but he seemed to think it was his position to cook for us." Steve and Tim remember breakfasts of doughy pancakes, or cornflakes and evaporated milk mixed with water. And breakfast was the best meal of the day! Lunches were usually peanut butter and onion sandwiches, which always prompted a frantic effort to dispose of the onions out of Truman's view. Dinners were often his infamous chicken-back soup—chicken backs boiled to death in a pot with 25 cloves of garlic, onions, tons of ground pepper, and unpeeled carrots. Other dinners included boiled ham hocks—plain—and a fairly acceptable attempt at chili.

Truman never asked the two what they wanted to eat, nor did he seem to notice their envious glances at the cats, who were usually getting hamburger. He seemed oblivious to his shortcomings as a chef. Truman would always watch them eat and say, "Hey, that's pretty damn good. You kids are livin' high off the hog. You wouldn't get this type of chow down at the Hilton."

The boys could only agree and look forward to Dayle's frequent visits, since she always brought a big pot roast. Truman was pleased to see her, and the pot roast, too, but he always hovered around her in the kitchen as she fixed it. "Now use the pressure cooker and cook it like Eddie used to," he'd say. "That's the way, that's the way Eddie did it."

Life for the boat boys was often like it was for the tens of young people who had worked summers at the resort. They had to be well versed in the rental charges for the boats—by then $5 for the first hour for motorboats and $3 each additional hour, $7.50 a day for rowboats, and $10 a day for canoes. But Truman had long since stopped taking tours of the lake in his motor launches. He sold one and never bothered to put the other back in the water.

Steve and Tim lived upstairs on the second floor of the boathouse and their off-duty hours gave them plenty of time to get involved in mischief, in the tradition of boat boys past. Once they found an old stump floating in the lake and decided it would make a nifty table for their room. In the process of hefting the massive stump up the narrow stairway, they broke the railing and the door. When he heard all the commotion, Truman trotted down to the boathouse and was furious at the damage done. But he was also impressed by the boys' resourcefulness in getting the huge stump up to the second floor and couldn't help but inquire how they had done it. "Ingenuity, Truman, ingenuity—just what you taught us," replied Tim, as Truman harumphed off.

The boat boys were supposed to wash their clothes and themselves in the bracing waters of Spirit Lake—a painful process of jumping in, jumping out, soaping up, jumping in, and jumping out. Whenever Truman went to town, the boys would head straight for the basement apartment below the restaurant, where they would languish for hours in a hot shower.

Truman loved to play tricks on the boat boys and they soon learned not to turn their backs on him when bailing out the boats because he would likely shove them into the lake. One night Tim was burning trash and he heard a rustling in the bushes. "Get your ass out of the bushes, Truman," he said. But when Tim grabbed a stick and decided to confront Truman, he turned the corner in the dark, and came face-to-face with a giant bear. Tim dropped the stick and raced to the lodge to tell Truman, who went outside calling, "Oh bear, come here bear! Oh that's a good bear!" Tim watched in amazement as the bear, about seven feet tall, rocked onto its hind legs while Truman stood about fifteen feet from it, chattering away. "I think the bear knew Truman," Tim recalls, "because it just looked at him, sniffed the air, got down on all fours and walked away."

Truman's well-honed ornery streak still ran deep. The staff at the Forest Service Visitors' Information Center by the campground was used to getting complaints about Truman. Usually the complaints were about Truman running people off his property—to which the Forest Service staff could only laugh and reply, "That's Harry." As one friend recalled, "He'd throw you out of his place two or three times to see how you bounced before he became friendly."

Truman often sent prospective customers the mile down the road to the Spirit Lake Lodge, which had been sold by the Gustafsons and taken over by Dave and Mariam Smith; it was run by their son Rob, whom Truman had known since he was three. Truman turned to kiddingly calling the lodge Hippieville because of young Smith and some of his friends. Other times Truman referred to it as a Peyton Place. "Go on down to Hippieville," Truman would tell people. "They've got gas down there, they've got everything you need down there. They've got toilet paper, fishing poles, they've got ice cream. I don't have shit around here. I've just got boats and cabins, boats and cabins; that's all I've got."

Truman's bluster was part show but he was also wary of strangers—and he had good reason to be. For years he had had customers leave without paying for boats. Others stole things—everything from canoes to boats to motors. Once his pickup truck was stolen, which sent him off on a cross-country pursuit of the culprits, and another time two young men with long hair had surprised him and Eddie in the lodge and pistol-whipped Truman and tied up Eddie while searching for money. From then on, Truman kept guns handy, and hippies were added to his "shit list," along with Republicans and young children and old people.

Even at 80, Truman had little use for old people, saying, "Those goddamn old people with no teeth in their heads, all they've got is their aches and complaints. They need somebody to push them around in a goddamn wheelchair."

That first summer after Eddie died—1976—Truman was again devastated by the death of someone he loved. His best friend Chickaloon Lund, who had done so much of the work at the lodge and at Prindle, became sick in the spring. Truman visited Chickaloon at his home in Castle Rock. But when Chickaloon's condition worsened and he had to be transferred to the hospital, Truman couldn't face seeing his friend wasting away in a hospital bed, so

he sent him flowers. Chickaloon died on June 24, at age
76, and after the funeral Truman hugged his wife Margaret and just cried and cried. It was the first time she
realized how much Chickaloon had meant to Truman.

With both Eddie and Chickaloon gone, it was only natural
that Truman would turn to someone else for friendship and
companionship That someone soon was young Rob Smith
of the Spirit Lake Lodge, who was the only other year-
round resident in the area along with Truman and Jim and
Pauline Lund. Rob was only 20 when he started managing
the rustic log lodge and he had high hopes and plans for the
day when he would buy it from his parents. He had always
been in love with the outdoors and he considered running
the lodge a great escape from his previous job in a sawmill.
Rob had long been in awe of Truman and he admired his
salty independence and his industrious hard work. But the
Truman he found was so lost and lonely that he sometimes
had a hard time believing it was the same man he had
looked up to as a boy.

Rob started visiting Truman at his lodge, and their
friendship soon grew until the handsome, soft-spoken
young man with the long hair became the son that Truman
had never had. "Nobody knew Harry better than Robbie in
his last days," recalls friend George Bowers. "Truman took
Robbie everyplace." But Rob saw some potential dangers in
their friendship and told Truman straight out: "I don't
want to just sit around and talk and have a few drinks. Now
look, Harry, I enjoy visiting you, but if you want me to come
up here, let's do something. When I'm up here, I want to
help you." Which he did. The two made things together
down at the boathouse, homemade parts for the snow
blower and other equipment. They'd conspire to befuddle
customers with phony information and send them shuttling
back and forth between the two lodges. They'd go on wood-
cutting expeditions—or wood bees, as they called them. In
the winter, they'd go out in the woods in the deep snow and
Rob would haul the wood on a toboggan. Jim Lund often

would join them and he and Rob would do the cutting while Truman would bring beer and cheese and crackers and watch from his perch on the tailgate of his truck.

"If there wasn't any risk involved," Rob recalls, "Truman created one, to make things interesting." Truman introduced him to his long-standing game of stealing rock from the Forest Service's gravel pit. They'd take truckloads at a time, racing one another to see who could load his truck first, and use the rock on their pathways and parking lots. They never got caught. Their last winter together at Spirit Lake, they even came up with a grand plan to steal an entire 20-foot pile of gravel.

Rob often picked up Truman's mail and brought him groceries. He also brought meals up from his lodge and Truman came to appreciate Rob's devotion. He never asked for or wanted anything in return for his kindness.

Rob provided no greater service to Truman than during his frequent injuries. After Eddie died, those injuries turned increasingly serious but Truman remained suspicious of doctors and hospitals. He kept a steadfast rule: he would not stay overnight at a hospital, no matter how serious the injury. He was afraid of theft and that vandals would damage the lodge if he left it unoccupied.

Truman's first serious injury after Eddie died was in the fall of 1975. He was out cutting wood and fell down an embankment, breaking his ankle. "Truman went into the hospital for three different casts during the first two weeks because they weren't comfortable and he didn't like them," Rob recalls. "After about three weeks, he tore off the third cast and built one of his own out of cardboard, rubber bands, and tape."

Another time Truman was washing his jeans and walked out on the back porch to throw away the tub of wash water and he ended up throwing himself off the porch as well. He fell down the back stairs and onto the concrete landing where he hit his head and knocked himself out. He was out about an hour—lying on the snow in the five-degree weather while wearing only his green T-shirt, Jockey shorts, and house slippers. Tim Hambleton was aghast the next morning when he saw Truman—with a dislocated shoulder, black eye, a knot on his head, and his elbow all skinned up. But Tim had to enlist all the persuasive help of Rob Smith, Jim Lund, and Skamania deputy sheriff George Barker before they could convince Truman to see a doctor. And once he was at St. John's Hospital in Longview, Truman was hardly the model patient. He gave his room to someone else and was wandering the halls, but nevertheless the doctor did examine him. Truman told Barker, "George, I don't like the son-of-a-bitch; he's so dry that when he farts, he crackles." The nurses headed for the doors.

Truman had two more serious injuries in the winter of 1978. He was cutting down a tree when the top fell on his head. Barker found him knocked out in the woods by the Duck Bay Road and checked his vital signs. But again Truman refused to go to the hospital, so Barker took him back to his lodge. Rob Smith again tried to help out. "I walked in and asked him, 'What's the matter, Harry?'" he recalls. "He said, 'Oh God, I just scratched myself up a bit. Fix her right up, would you, kid?'"

Rob said he'd do what he could, but as soon as he pulled back the bandage, blood started to spurt from the deep gash. Truman kept insisting that Rob could fix it up. He finally let Rob take him to the hospital.

Truman made no protest that same winter when he was reaching to pull some snow out of the chute of his snow blower and his hand got caught by the blade, tearing the flesh off three of his fingers. "It was really bad and the doctors told him in no way could he ever use those fingers again," says Rob. "They thought they might have to amputate them or definitely do some plastic surgery with skin grafts. But Harry told them, 'Stitch them up the best you can, I'm going home.' So they did. He was in tears, squeezing my hand tight. They had deadened the fingers, but he could still feel it. I changed the dressing on those fingers regularly and he worked on them. He said the pain was one of the worst he'd ever experienced. But those fingers healed. There were no fingernails on them when the skin healed across, but they worked all right."

Even the assistance of Lloyd Sverdrup, Truman's accountant, was required after one of his injuries. Truman fell off the roof of the lodge when he was shoveling snow and broke his leg. A claim was filed with the Department of Labor and Industries Industrial Insurance Division—since shoveling snow off the roofs was absolutely essential to keep them from caving in—and Lloyd handled the claim.

Truman had to be examined by a doctor prior to an appeal-board hearing and he received a stern lecture from the physician. "You're a damn fool," the doctor said. "A man your age shouldn't be up on the roof working in the first place." Truman snapped, "Damn it! Look, I'm 80 years old and at 80, I have the right to make up my mind and do what I want to do!"

Truman went into the examination claiming a 20-percent disability. After the exam, the doctor increased it to 30 percent, and Truman was later awarded about $2,000 by the state. Truman of course thought the payment should have been much more.

10:

Under the Volcano

MARCH 20, 1980, must have dawned like any other morning for Truman. In my mind, I can see him waking up early and instinctively reaching across the bed for Auntie Eddie, as he had so many mornings since she had died. I can see him again cursing the fact that he hadn't died first and then I can see him telling himself for the thousandth time, "Quit feeling sorry for yourself, you old son-of-a-bitch." Then he'd swat Dolly, Auntie Eddie's favorite cat, with a gruff pat and scramble out of bed, get dressed and go downstairs.

Truman would peer outside and see the fresh snow and think how much work there was to be done. He'd hope that Rob Smith would come up with some mail.

Truman would have padded down the basement stairs, picked up a piece of pitch and some wood from the pile on the floor, and tossed them into the still-smoldering embers in the ancient furnace. Then he'd go back upstairs to face the task of fixing some breakfast — yet another reminder of how lonely he had been for these last few years. He really did hate to cook for himself and eat alone — that was really one of the worst things of all — so that morning he decided just to drink a big glass of buttermilk for breakfast. What he hated most was that there was no backside to swat affectionately, no one to tease, no one to complain to about the weather.

Except his cats, all 16 of them. He'd feed them some dry food and refill their water dishes—all the while chattering constantly to them as if they understood every word he said and would respond at any minute.

That afternoon, Truman was outside involved in his never-ending chore of shoveling snow when the earth shook slightly at 3:45 P.M. He immediately thought that the warming spring weather had loosened an avalanche down the sides of Mount St. Helens, as frequently happened at that time of year.

What Truman certainly didn't think then was that the mountain was springing back to life as a volcano after 123 years of quiet serenity. Nor did he think that his loneliness was about to end and his life of routine at the lodge was about to change in ways he couldn't possibly imagine. He was about to begin an emotional roller-coaster ride that would last eight very long weeks.

But at the same time that Truman was shoveling snow, seismographs at the University of Washington in Seattle and elsewhere recorded an earthquake centered 20 miles north of Mount St. Helens. It measured a moderate 4.1 on the Richter Scale, but its location so close to the mountain gave scientists cause for concern.

Those concerns intensified during the next few days, as did the earthquakes. They became more and more frequent, and three days later were being recorded at a rate of 40 an hour. The quakes were closer to the mountain, too. A 4.4 quake on March 24 sent avalanches rolling down the mountain's north face up above Spirit Lake and for the first time, visitors were urged to stay away from Mount St. Helens.

The potential seriousness of the situation prompted federal, state, and local officials to meet on March 26 and consider possible evacuation plans. That same day, the Forest Service closed the area above the timber line because of the recurring earthquakes and avalanches.

Excitement was building about a possible eruption, but government scientists downplayed the possibility. Don Mullineaux, a geologist with the U.S. Geological Survey, had reassuring words for reporters that day. He discussed Mount St. Helens's past volcanic history and concluded that if the mountain erupted, it would be what he called "a small eruptive event" with most of its effects limited to the mountain's slopes.

Truman, too, encountered reporters that Wednesday. They had been sent Truman's way by his friend Chuck Tonn of the Forest Service. "Go visit Truman over at his lodge," Tonn advised, "he'll give your stories some color."

Truman didn't disappoint them. He was the kind of crusty codger journalists love—a real character—and his language was saltier than a sailor's. The only problem was trying to keep up with his runaway mouth. A tape recorder was almost essential.

"I'm the only one up here," Truman said that day. "If the son-of-a-bitch blows, all they've got to do is find me. I'm not going to leave." Within 24 hours, the mountain did just that. Shortly after noon, a loud boom was heard throughout much of the area and Mount St. Helens spit a plume of ash thousands of feet into the atmosphere. Deputy sheriff George Barker was manning the roadblock on the Spirit Lake Highway, and his radio crackled with orders to evacuate everyone. He immediately took off for Spirit Lake, red lights flashing and siren screaming.

Truman had been enjoying a quiet conversation with Rob Smith and Kathy Paulson, Rob's girlfriend, when "all of a sudden the whole building seemed like a little cardboard box, rocking back and forth," Rob remembers. They went out on the front porch to see what was going on and soon Barker's patrol car raced up. "Everybody out!" his loudspeaker boomed. "The mountain's erupting! Clear the area!" Then Barker raced off to the Forest Service work center. The porch continued to shake and Rob and Kathy quickly prepared to leave. But they couldn't convince Truman to come along with them.

"We tried hard to get Harry to leave," Rob recalls. "We told him we'd take him down to his place at Prindle. We said we could go clean the place up, as we'd been planning to, and we said it's a good time to leave, with the roadblocks up." Truman wasn't convinced. He was worried about leaving his lodge unguarded and he couldn't really believe that there was all that much danger from the mountain. He might have been much more convinced if he had been present a couple hours later when a young geologist named David Johnston held a briefing for reporters at the turnaround up at the timber line.

The ground continued to shake as the 30-year-old Geological Survey scientist in the lumberjack shirt and the watchcap said calmly: "It is extremely dangerous where we are standing. If the mountain exploded, we would die. It's like standing next to a dynamite keg with the fuse lit — only we don't know how long that fuse is."

Mount St. Helens was much changed on March 27. A small crater appeared on the summit, 250 feet in diameter and 150 feet deep, surrounded by a dirty black ring of ash on the snow. That day's eight earthquakes also left large fissures more than a mile long on the north side of the mountain. Truman could see the cracks through his binoculars and he was scared.

The trickle of scientists and reporters, which had started to build with the mountain's first stirrings, turned to a flood after March 27. Eventually all the reporters learned to make the required stop at Truman's lodge to pick up the quotes that would make their stories sing.

At first this presented a real dilemma for Truman. He was a man who always loved being the center of attention and had long enjoyed a lion's share of local notoriety, but he had always refused requests for interviews, even from folks he considered friends, like the McClelland family who owned the nearby *Daily News* of Longview. He was sorely tempted by the reporters' repeated requests, because he knew publicity could only help his business. One of the few times he had ever given in was in 1952 for an article written about the resort in the Sunday *Seattle Times*.

Usually, though, whenever Truman would get the itch to talk, Eddie had interceded. "Truman, if you talk to those damn reporters," she would say, "all your skeletons are going to come falling out of the closet." And he could only agree. There was rum-running and moonshining in his past, and there was something that happened in California that so scared him he hid all the way up in the wilderness at Spirit Lake. That was why he wouldn't allow close-up pictures taken by other than family and friends.

But Eddie was gone when Mount St. Helens began to rumble, and Truman was a lonely man who found the reporters' attention invigorating after too much time spent alone. And at 83, he figured, he had probably outlived anyone who might have been carrying a grudge from back in the 1920s.

So one morning, Truman woke up and said to himself, "Hell, I'll make up to those reporters; I'll make up with every newspaper, every television and radio station in the United States." He decided he would put on a show for them. His past would be part of an open book — bootlegging and all. Why, he'd even pour them a Schenley's and Coke if they wanted one.

But Truman was not doing this just to be kind. He was a wily manipulator with a well-refined talent for getting what he wanted. For one thing, the reporters would help keep his mind off the frequent earthquakes, which rattled the big lodge and prompted him to say, "You know, I am scared as hell about earthquakes; I just wish it would stop all the shaking." More importantly, Truman figured the press could help him escape if there were a big eruption. So many of the news crews flew over the roadblocks and into his resort by helicopter that the highway in front of the lodge often resembled a landing pad. Truman could just see a

news helicopter swooping in to rescue him at the first report
of any lava flowing down the mountain. Some of the reporters had promised to do just that—a fair trade for a
great scoop.

Truman figured that putting up with the reporters' ques-
tions was a small price to pay for such an insurance policy.
Besides, the reporters were good listeners and fun to be
around. Several would become Truman's friends. One of
the first major stories on him was in the *Daily News* of
Longview—whose interview requests he had long spurned.
The March 29 edition carried almost a full-page story on
Truman and a picture showing him stroking his tomcat, Old
Red.

Truman said what he would repeat countless times in the
coming weeks. "I've walked that mountain for 50 years. I
know her. If it erupts with lava, it's not going to get me at
Spirit Lake. Those geologists might know something about
the inside of a mountain, but I know her contours. Besides,
if I left this place, it would worry me to death. If this place is
gonna go, I want to go with it. 'Cause if I lost it, it would kill
me in a week anyway."

Truman was so pleased with the article and the picture
that he proudly showed the photograph to Old Red several
times and would say later, "Red really liked that picture."
Articles in far bigger newspapers soon followed and Truman was well on his way to becoming the only person at
Mount St. Helens known throughout the nation. Truman
was on the front page of the *San Francisco Examiner* on
Sunday, March 30, and the next day he made the *New York
Times,* complete with the picture of him and Old Red. Truman couldn't have been prouder, and he kept the *New York
Times* article close at hand to show his visitors; he felt it made
him a certified national celebrity.

The only problem with Truman's new-found fame was
the headaches it was causing for law-enforcement officials
charged with keeping people out of the forbidden Red Zone
around the mountain. "The main pressure of people want-

ing to go in was not necessarily to see the mountain, but to interview Truman," deputy George Barker recalls. "He was the drawing card."

The roadblock on the Spirit Lake Highway quickly became a bureaucratic nightmare. The State Highway Department didn't feel it had the authority to close the highway, so the responsibility fell to the sheriffs in Cowlitz and Skamania counties, through which the road ran. They established round-the-clock roadblocks, which were effective in draining their overtime budgets but were largely ineffective in keeping people out. Later the Highway Department installed barricades and the State Patrol manned them.

The pressure to interview Truman grew as the earthquakes and avalanches continued and lightning bolts, some two miles long, flashed above the mountain. A second crater was spotted on the summit and blue flames could be seen in both. Since the press was doing all it could to skirt the roadblocks and get to Truman, the solution of law-enforcement officials was to bring Truman outside the prohibited area and have him hold a press conference. A date was set for Sunday, March 30, and the place was to be the Toutle Lake School.

A cadre of top officers from the two counties assembled at the school and a four-wheel-drive pickup was dispatched to fetch Truman from his lodge. It was driven by deputy Barker, who Truman had come to consider "my own deputy." This red-carpet treatment was heady stuff for Truman, as was the gaggle of reporters waiting for him at the school. Seattle and Portland newspapers and broadcast stations had sent crews, as had United Press International and *The National Geographic.* Truman didn't let them down. He was in rare form, wearing his green plaid Pendleton jacket over a tattered green sweatshirt and his red baseball cap with the number seven tilted back on his head at a jaunty angle.

He began the press conference with instructions to "shoot me head on, boys; don't shoot me from the side." He told about the earthquakes the day before and their effect on his lodge: "We had a show yesterday morning, boys. It rolled my bed clear across the room and I decided it was time to get up. It woke me up about five. It's a thrill, a strange sensation. I'd love it if I wasn't scared to death." With arms flailing for emphasis, he told about his four-week supply of food and formidable stock of Schenley's. "Don't think my red cheeks are caused by fresh mountain air," he laughed. "That's a Schenley flush."

He told about his homemade remedy to fix what ailed the mountain: "If I'd had anything to do with it, I'd have dropped a bomb right down in the middle of it. It would have blown every goddamn thing out, ice would have filled the hole and it would have been over all at once." That morning there had been a new eruption, which blew a cloud of ash as far as 150 miles away, south to Bend, Oregon. But Truman pooh-poohed the predictions of geologists who said the worst was yet to come, and he poked fun at the scientists themselves. "The mountain has shot its wad and it hasn't hurt my place a bit," he said. "But those goddamn geologists with hair down to their butts wouldn't pay no attention to ol' Truman. I don't think they know any more about the inside of that mountain than I do—and I don't know nothing about the inside of her."

For more than an hour, Truman regaled the crowd of reporters, deputies, and onlookers—which totaled about 40 people—with tall tales of his 54 years at Spirit Lake. And he made it clear he was going to stay at Mount St. Helens Lodge no matter what. "You couldn't pull me out with a mule team," he said. "That mountain's part of Truman and Truman's part of that mountain."

Before he left, he invited everyone to come visit him at the lodge during the summer and admonished them to "bring your checkbooks and some rotgut; don't forget the rotgut." Then he motioned to the deputies that it was time to take him home. "OK, you buzzards," he waved to the beguiled press corps, "I'll see you in church."

It was all vintage Truman. Deputy Barker had watched and laughed with everyone else in the crowd. But Barker was also becoming concerned about the 83-year-old man and the effects this attention was having. Barker wasn't sure he liked what he was seeing in his friend. "Harry was a Truman I didn't know; he was a man thriving on publicity," Barker recalls. "He was full of jokes, but in retrospect, that was his way of letting off nervousness."

Other longtime friends came to feel the same way about Truman, including Chuck Tonn of the Forest Service. He and Karen Jacobsen—a young Forest Service back country ranger whom Truman had first kidded about having "a bikini and a badge" and later had come to respect—had celebrated New Year's Eve with Truman in his lodge. In March, the two were ordered to leave the area along with other Forest Service people. "Harry was in a different frame of mind during the period of the eruption," Tonn remembers. "He was afraid, and like you do when you're afraid, he talked a lot more and boasted a lot more."

Friend Rob Smith came to feel that the fear and the uncertainty were also making Truman drink more. Despite his pack trip revels with friends like Garrity and Douglas, Truman was usually a moderate drinker who mixed himself less Schenley's and more Coke as the night wore on.

Those of us in his own family had little sense of that. Everyone was keeping in touch, telling each other whenever Truman was on television. We looked forward to the arrival of the day's papers, and friends from other parts of the state clipped articles from their newspapers and sent them to us. We had all always thought Truman was a bona fide character and now everyone else in the country was finding that out, too. But our excitement about Truman becoming a national celebrity was always tinged with very real fears for his safety and worries about what Mount St. Helens might do.

On April 2, strong earthquakes—registering 4.5 and 4.7 on the Richter Scale—rocked the mountain. Harmonic tremors indicated that molten rock was moving further up from deep inside the volcano. On April 3, an even stronger quake of 4.8 occurred and Washington Governor Dixy Lee Ray declared a state of emergency and ordered the National Guard to control the growing hordes of sightseers.

Truman was staying put, looking a television reporter straight in the eye and saying, "Hell, it would take an act of God or three acts of Congress to get me off that mountain—and we both know how slow Congress is." But out of the camera's eye, Truman was an emotional wreck— scared by the earthquakes which jolted his lodge, and frightened by conflicting predictions from scientists who Truman thought were supposed to know what a volcano would do.

Rob stayed at nearby Spirit Lake Lodge for a couple nights during the earthquakes, and he had more than his fill of what his friend Truman was going through every night. "I think Harry was just petrified," Rob recalls. "He stayed pretty much under the weather during that time and he was going through a lot more whiskey. When I stayed overnight at our lodge, I could understand why. I couldn't sleep because there was so much going through my mind. Then I'd just get to sleep and I'd hear a few dishes go clink, clink, clink and then the whole building would start moving. It was just the little noise of the dishes that would bring it to my attention and my heart would start going boom, boom, boom. I could just see the lava coming. It was dark and raining and snowing and blowing and I'd look out the door where I'd parked my truck right at the edge of the road heading down the hill. I didn't even sleep in my bed, but on the couch by the fireplace because I was afraid to go upstairs to sleep. Then I'd lay down and fall asleep and the same thing would happen every 20 minutes."

Alone in his lodge and with no way to communicate with the outside world, Truman was a lonely, frightened man. His friend George Bowers, the used-car dealer, saw that when he stopped by the lodge to visit on Friday, April 4.

Truman proudly led George into the kitchen where stacks of mail covered every counter and shelf. George couldn't believe the deluge of letters that Truman was receiving and he joked that he ought to get a press secretary. "I'll tell you, they're going to bury me up here all right, with all this damn fan mail," Truman said. "I couldn't answer all that mail in a year. By God, if this keeps up the U.S. is going to have to run a special mail truck up here for poor ol' Truman."

Then he had George read some of the letters aloud to him. Many came from women from all across the country, saying they wanted to come visit. One even wrote that she was a healthy woman, a good housekeeper, and an outdoors girl that would make Truman a good wife. She said she was going to come out and meet him and if he liked her, she'd just stay. "I wrote that old biddy fast and told her to stay put," Truman said. "Goddamn it, I don't need anybody out here; I'm happy the way I am. So I wrote her and told her, 'You stay there!'" George thought that was so funny that he made mental plans to get together with Rob Smith and pull a practical joke on Truman. George would dress up like a woman, complete with wig and falsies, and Rob would accompany "her" to Truman's where he would say that he just didn't have the heart to turn her away. Then George would start chasing Truman around the lodge. It was a great plan, but one they never got around to putting into action.

George was reading the letters until his voice turned hoarse, but when he tried to quit, Truman would plead, "Just one more letter, George. Do you need more light? Read me another one." Then Truman would pad off and mix them another Schenley's and Coke. This went on for hours and when George finally got up to go, Truman turned angry, not wanting the evening with a friend to end.

"OK, you son-of-a-bitch, get to the door, get the hell out of here," Truman snapped. "I don't ever want to see you again—git!" George sensed Truman's hurt. But Truman quickly said, "No, have another drink, read another letter."

That was when George started to read the letters from the
children in Vicki Weiss's fifth-grade class at Indian Hill
School in Grand Blanc, Michigan.

As George read letter after letter, Truman started to cry.
The tears ran down his cheeks. When he read the very last
one, Truman said, "Those kids are America; they are the
core of the country. There's not a bad one in the bunch. I
sure would like to do something for them." George suggested sending the class a can of volcanic ash for a fund-
raising project. Truman at first refused, saying that the
mountain itself would probably send ash all the way to
Michigan one of these days. But George reminded Truman
that little packets of ash were selling for $2 each at souvenir
stands, and Truman finally agreed. Later, George sent the
kids a coffee can full of ash with a letter from Truman.

While George was still there, the building started to rock
and the cats raised their backs and Truman's barometer
hanging by the kitchen window started to swing back and
forth. George was terrified, but Truman boasted, "By God,
it's swinging pretty good. That damn mountain knocked
me clean out of bed the other night."

"You've got to get out of here, Harry," George said. "Dig
up that damn money you've got stashed and go down to
your other place at Prindle. Goddamn it, Harry, this thing
could get bad. Hell, the law will watch this place for you."
Truman was unconvinced. "Listen," he said. "If an asshole
like you can get up here, anyone could." George glanced
down at his watch, which read almost 2 A.M. He was surprised and shocked by the finality of what Truman said
next. "If I die tomorrow," Truman said, "I've had a damn
good life. I've done everything I could do and I've done
everything I ever wanted to do."

Then George said goodbye and walked outside, where he
stuck his face in a snowbank to sober up. He got in his
pickup and headed down the highway. He was almost near
Silver Lake when he applied the brakes and got the fright
of his life—the loudest cat's scream he had ever heard.

George stopped the truck and found one of Truman's own cats had stowed away and was hiding under the brake pedal. The next morning, George decided to run an ad in the *Daily News* of Longview to see if he could find a volunteer willing to take Truman's cat back to him. But the newspaper, ever eager for yet another Truman story, decided to run a news story about the cat. The story didn't turn up any volunteers, but George was spooked when a woman's voice told him over the phone, "You know, that cat leaving the mountain is a bad omen. I don't think you should take that cat back up there. Little creatures have a sense of fear. You shouldn't make it go back!"

George himself returned to Truman's with the cat on Easter Sunday, April 6—just in time to see the large helicopter land, carrying the NBC-TV crew that was to film an interview for the Today Show. Truman was soon in fine TV form, introducing him as his "old sidekick," pouring Schenley's all around. He sat at the antique player piano and put on a few rolls—something he simply wouldn't do for several years after Eddie died.

While Truman was entertaining reporters at his resort, a debate was raging in the Skamania and Cowlitz county courthouses about Truman's status as the only person allowed to stay within the Red Zone. Much of the responsibility for letting Truman stay at his lodge seemed to rest on the shoulders of William Closner, the sheriff of Skamania County, where the lodge was located. "Truman wasn't a problem himself, but his staying there had been a total hassle," Closner recalls. "I checked with our prosecutor and he said he doubted he could get an impartial jury to hear the case and therefore he doubted we could prosecute Truman. Besides, we did not feel it was in his best interest and there was no way to avoid bad publicity if we did."

Deputy Ben Bena of Cowlitz County felt much the same way. "There wasn't a law-enforcement official in the country who would have arrested Harry. He was at his own home, and there was the matter of his age and the number of years he had made that his home. And at that time, we weren't absolutely sure what the mountain was going to do."

On that Easter Sunday, geologist Mullineaux had said the probability was "very, very low in terms of a big eruption." Two days later, the two craters atop the summit of Mount St. Helens merged into one—a massive gash 1,700 feet across and 850 feet deep. The longest eruption yet spilled forth from 8:22 A.M. until 2 P.M. But the U.S. Forest Service and the U.S. Geological Survey issued a joint statement that day which said, "All these observations imply that there is no indication that a major eruption of molten rock will occur in the near future."

The mountain turned surprisingly quiet for more than two weeks. There were no harmonic tremors and some local people began to think that the mountain, which the Indians had called Fire Mountain, had indeed gone back to sleep. A few ventured back into the Red Zone after signing waivers, news briefings dropped from three a day to every other day, and Truman moved his bed back upstairs.

The spring air was heavy with a sense of relief. Normal routines returned. Truman fed his birds and cats and raccoons. He traveled a mile down the highway where he made sure Jim and Pauline Lund's rustic home was safe—even putting a padlock on the door—and he went across the road to check on the Smiths' Spirit Lake Lodge. Truman relished his role as guardian of the mountain while the others were gone, and it didn't particularly bother him that Jim Lund didn't have a key for the padlock.

But Truman continued to be very worried about the possibility of vandalism and thefts. Not only had Truman been assaulted and robbed, but several of his favorite animals—a bear, a doe, mink, otter, and beaver—had been shot dead in recent years. "The only thing I've got to worry about is the goddamn two-legged animal," Truman told the *National Geographic*'s Fred Stocker. "That son-of-a-bitch is going to stick a knife in you at night and rob you. That's the only son-of-a-bitch you've got to worry about in this world—not the wild animals. You treat them right and let them alone and they'll never bother you. They're your friends, but those two-legged son-of-a-bitches that we're living with today who call themselves human beings are the rottenest goddamn scum of the earth."

Now the area was in the news every day and people were coming to the area from all over the world. Trouble seemed sure to follow. Truman knew full well that the law-enforcement officials simply couldn't keep people out of the area. There were 8,000 miles of trails and logging roads in the region, and sportsmen's maps showing them all were for sale in practically any store.

Truman frequently heard cars come up the supposedly closed road around midnight and he would tell deputy Barker, "I would go out in the garage sometimes and just wait for them to bust through the door. I'd even sleep in the car sometimes." Truman stayed up late at night, leaving lights on and prowling around on the lookout for anything out of the ordinary. His fears proved founded when the Spirit Lake Lodge was broken into and vandalized. Mariam Smith, Rob's mother, remembers what she found after the vandals left. "They went through our lodge with a fine-tooth comb. My God, we got up there and every bed had been slept in, the deep fryer was on, they stole all our candy, all the cigarettes, all the food and anything they could get their hands on. And we had stayed away like good people, like we'd been asked to. But they weren't patrolling the area."

During Mount St. Helens's April lull, the visits by the news helicopters became far less frequent, so Truman was particularly happy to see a team from one of his favorite newspapers—the *Oregonian*, in Portland. He looked at the mountain through his ever-present binoculars and told them, "I know that mountain like the wrinkles on my hand and can spot a gnat moving on it with these glasses." Truman proceeded to give the reporter and photographers an earthquake lesson, using his homemade version of the

Richter Scale. He explained that he could gauge the sever-
ity of an earthquake by how much it moved the Rainier
Beer sign hanging in the main room in the lodge. If it hit
the wall, it was a number-five quake. He had a similar
system in the kitchen where the measuring devices were
his barometer and the Christmas balls which would clank
against the window panes. Truman closed the interview,
as he usually did, with his pledge to stay at his lodge: "I
been livin' up here with the mountain and the lake for 54
years. I'd die if I left—just fold up and die. They keep my
heart going."

But on April 20—only four days after the *Oregonian*
published a full page on him—Truman did indeed leave.
The rumblings of Mount St. Helens and the earthquakes
couldn't convince him to do that, but a retirement party for
his best friend John Garrity could. Garrity's party had long
been planned for April 21 in St. Paul, and Truman had
already written his regrets, saying, "You know I'd love to be
there but I can't because of the mountain. But at 5:30 P.M.
St. Paul time, I'll be drinking a toast to you, by God!" Garrity
understood, but Truman was still nagged by the thought of
missing such an event and he told Rob Smith how much he
wanted to go. Rob replied that he should go, and offered to
drive Truman to the airport. Truman finally agreed, but
only if Rob would fly to Minnesota with him.

Truman locked up his lodge tight and sneaked out a
secret way. Then they flew out of Seattle the day of Garrity's
party, buying their tickets with money which Rob remembered "smelled moldy." Truman was beside himself with
excitement on the big jet and he couldn't resist the chance to
let the pretty young stewardesses know who he was. He
called them each Honey as he happily signed autographs.

They arrived unannounced at the airport that afternoon
and called Truman's other Minnesota friend, Doc Peterson,
who picked them up. Garrity was in the receiving line at the
St. Paul Athletic Club shaking hands at the appointed hour
when Truman was supposed to toast him at Spirit Lake. But

instead, a hunched-over figure sneaked up behind him and enveloped him in a mighty bear hug. Truman had sprung his surprise and made his million-dollar entrance.

"It fills me up just to remember that moment," Garrity said weeks later. "He told me, 'I would have flown all the way to the Hi-waiian Islands or seven times across the U.S.A. to come to this goddamn party.'"

The celebrity from Mount St. Helens was the star of the party, going from group to group, from the chairman of the board of Burlington Northern on down, introducing Rob as his "bouncer, bodyguard, and babysitter."

"This is my young man Smith with me," Truman said. "He's takin' the place of Eddie, looking after me and watching out for me."

But throughout the party and the long night of celebrating and reminiscing at Doc Peterson's that followed, Truman remained concerned about what might be happening to his lodge. Garrity and Peterson wanted him and Rob to go north for some fishing, but Truman refused. He and Rob were back on a plane 24 hours after they had arrived.

The lodge was untouched when they returned and the mountain hadn't stirred. But two days later—on April 24—scientists announced an ominous new discovery. They had been comparing pictures taken a month before with new pictures and they had found a massive bulge growing on Mount St. Helens's north face, 8,000 feet up the mountain at the head of the Forsyth Glacier. The bulge was two-thirds of a mile wide and 300 feet out, and expanding at the rate of five feet a day.

The earthquakes soon resumed—more than 30 a day—and by April 30, the scientists had agreed that the growing bulge represented "the most serious potential hazard posed by current volcanic activity." That same day, Governor Dixy Lee Ray declared that the Red Zone was to be finally drawn at 10 miles around the mountain, and scientists and law-enforcement officers were the only ones permitted inside. Violators would be subject to $500 fines and possible jail terms. There was no mention made of Truman. But he would be allowed to stay in his lodge, eight miles up the Spirit Lake Highway from where the final roadblock was located.

That same day, my sister Elaine flew down to Seattle from her home in Alaska. Mount St. Helens filled the newspapers there and so did stories about Truman. She was becoming increasingly anxious about his safety and about what he had told her the November before, when she had visited his lodge for the first time since Auntie Eddie died. In November, she was driving her daughter Corrine to Denver and they had had a delightful evening of reminiscing and playing the player piano with Truman. But Truman had startled her the next morning when they said goodbye and he told her, "Well, ya know kid, this will be the last time you'll see your ol' Uncle Harry. Yep, you'll never see Old Harry Truman again."

She wanted to make sure that wasn't the case, so on May 1, she set out for Spirit Lake accompanied by Stephen Gorringe, our nephew, and Patrick Mount, her brother-in-law. It took considerable persuasion for her to convince the National Guardsmen to let them through the roadblock.

They drove up to the lodge and walked in the back door where they saw Truman being interviewed under the bright lights of Seattle's KIRO-TV. When he spotted them, he shouted, "Jesus Christ, the family!" and scampered over. He pumped Stephen's hand hard and he told Elaine, "You didn't come all the way from Alaska just to see me; you must have had some business in Seattle." She could only nod her head in the affirmative, as the tears welled up in her eyes. After the TV crew left, Elaine gave Truman the two bottles of Schenley's she'd brought. He didn't open either bottle, but silently placed them in the cupboard, which was already filled with many bottles of Schenley's—gifts from reporters.

"It was a sweet thing for you to remember, but I'm not drinking now," Truman told her, adding that he had not

been feeling well. His illness didn't surprise her as much as
his not drinking. When she first arrived, Elaine concluded
that he looked tired and worn out, and his vivid blue eyes
seemed to have lost their spark, just as they had seemed
right after Auntie Eddie died.

While Elaine fried up the chicken she'd brought that
evening, Truman pored over his stacks of mail. She could
readily see that the letters from the children meant the most
to the man who had spent so much of his life disliking "little
buggers."

"Why would they draw pictures and send letters to an old
bastard like me?" he plaintively asked Elaine. "It brings tears
to my eyes every time I look at them."

Elaine then offered to help him answer a few of the
letters, but Truman refused. "No, I'll get to them shortly," he
said. "I want to do this myself, personally, so I can show
them how much I appreciate the cute little bastards' concern. But they needn't worry; I'm where I want to be."

The three visitors had thought they might end up spending the night at the lodge, as relatives always did when they
visited Truman. But he wouldn't allow it, even though the
hour was late. The mountain was much too dangerous, he
said, they had to get down the road to safer ground. So
they left.

Mount St. Helens, meanwhile, was springing back to
violent life. On May 7, there was the first major ash eruption
in more than two weeks. On May 8, there was a 5.0 earthquake; on May 9, another. That same day, the U.S. Geological Survey abandoned its observation camp at the timber
line, saying it was too dangerous; a new, presumably safer
camp was established on a ridge six miles from the mountain, and geologist David Johnston took his position there.

Law-enforcement officials were increasingly worried that
Truman should do the same thing himself. He had certainly
made his point and nobody could doubt his courage or his
convictions. What they might doubt, though, was his sanity
in staying steadfast in the shadow of that growing bulge on
the volcano's north face.

Those officials who knew Truman best—"his" deputy,
George Barker, Skamania sheriff William Closner, and
Cowlitz sheriff Les Nelson—were worried that Truman,
who had used the media so well, was now trapped by the
media image he himself had created. Other friends worried
the same thing. Friend George Bowers came to believe,
"After Truman had made such a big hullabaloo about staying up there and everything, he just sort of was forced into
it."

Lieutenant Bob Covington of the Cowlitz County
Sheriff's Department agrees: "I really feel that the news
people made Truman such a hero, and such a big thing out
of it, that he didn't want to lose face." And Truman himself
hinted at his dilemma when he told Jim Lund, "The only
reason I'm here is because they let me stay."

Sheriffs Closner and Nelson and deputy Barker decided
to have one more go at trying to persuade Truman to leave.
Perhaps if all three of them went together he would finally
listen to reason. And they did have what they considered to
be a pretty fair plan—they would take him down to Prindle
themselves and keep his leaving very hush-hush. The three
officers drove up to Truman's lodge on Saturday, May 10,
with their arguments well planned and their hopes high.
But almost as soon as they walked in the door, they could see
their joint effort was going to prove futile.

Truman was ecstatic. He had just received a letter praising
him from Governor Dixy Lee Ray and he was strutting
about waving his arms wildly with the letter in his hand. He
couldn't wait for each of them to read her letter which said:

> Your independence and straightforwardness is a fine
> example for all of us, particularly for senior citizens.
> When everyone else involved in the Mount St. Helens
> eruption appeared to be overcome by all the excite-
> ment, you stuck to what you knew and what common
> experience and sense told you. We could use a lot more
> of that kind of thinking, particularly in politics.
> I get a fair amount of criticism for calling things the

way I see them. I'm glad someone like yourself got credit for the same approach.

As far as the Republicans being responsible for the activity of the mountain, you may well be right. Hot air, steam, smoke, with no backbone seems to have always been their trademark.

Dixy Lee Ray

When all three finished reading the governor's letter, Truman said a hearty, "Damn right! She needs me on her staff." Truman was so excited by the letter that the three officers knew there was no way they could calm him down and persuade him to leave. But they tried anyway. They told him that the growing bulge on the mountain meant that it was likely to all come down right on top of him and he would certainly be killed. Truman scoffed at that, saying he had things all figured out. There was a hogback ridge between him and the mountain, he said, and that was his line of defense against the volcano. It would separate any ice and rock before it got to his lodge, forcing it below, where the main damage it might do would be washing out the highway.

"After the governor's letter, it seemed useless to try to get Harry to leave," Barker recalls. "Harry was more concerned at that time about how he should respond to the governor's letter, how he should address a letter to her."

Truman would have gotten far different advice from the mail that had arrived at George Bowers's the day before. They were a second set of letters sent by Truman's fifth-grade friends at Indian Hill School in Grand Blanc, Michigan. Teacher Vicki Weiss wrote and said that Truman's letter and coffee can of ash had arrived. The students, she said, "perked right up after that, were smiling and happy all day long. They LOVED hearing from you." She told about their plans to sell the ash at the school's science fair and about the model volcano the class was building, which they all called Harry's Mountain. All 28 students in the class had written

individual letters to Truman as well. They were full of
questions: How he could possibly keep track of 16 cats? Did
he have any children of his own? But unlike Governor Ray's
letter, the letters of the schoolchildren were filled with some
sincere fears for Truman's safety.

"Do you ever feel when you go to bed you may never wake
up?" wrote Matt Sherwood. "What's it like living on a volcanic mountain? What do you do? Aren't you worried it will
explode? If it does, you'll die, and we care about you!" wrote
Lee Ann Lott. "Your letter was so heartwarming some of
our eyes got watery. Your letters made everyone's day
worthwhile," wrote Elizabeth Goldner. "I think if it is not
safe up there, you should leave until it is. Because your life
is more important than any house or lodge ever is."

George Bowers knew how much these new letters would
mean to Truman. He planned to take them up to the lodge
on Sunday, May 18.

The bulge on Mount St. Helens was still growing and the
scientists now agreed that its cause was molten rock moving
up inside the mountain. But the scientists also acted to calm
the fears of area residents. Mullineaux of the Geological
Survey told an anxious group gathered at the Toutle Lake
School that a "large event" was still unlikely, that the north
face of the mountain probably wouldn't collapse all at once.

On May 12, another 5.0 earthquake rocked Mount St.
Helens—sending an 800-foot-wide avalanche skidding
3,000 feet down the mountain's north face. On that day, a
Seattle news crew had been in to interview Truman and
reported back to the Skamania County Sheriff's Department that he had been "in a broken-down and emotional
state" and wanted out at last. This set off a frantic but secret
search for a helicopter, while deputy Barker set off for
Truman's lodge. Two Cowlitz County deputies also drove
in. But when Barker arrived and went in to talk to Truman
alone, he was told in no uncertain terms that the report was
wrong—Truman still wanted to stay.

On Wednesday, May 14, Truman did fly out to safety, but

only briefly. He visited the children at Clear Lake Elementary School near Salem, Oregon, courtesy of a helicopter provided by the *National Geographic*. Truman had ridden in the *Geographic* helicopter before—hovering right over the crater in Mount St. Helens's summit—and he had become good friends with several members of the *Geographic* staff, who frequently restocked his supply of Schenley's. Truman had even introduced *Geographic* photographer Fred Stocker to one of his favorite reporters—Robin Anderson of Portland's KATU-TV—and they were married later that summer.

When Truman landed at the school, all 104 students stood outside cheering and holding banners which said, "Harry—We Love You!" Truman told them about his long life at Spirit Lake and why he wouldn't leave his lodge. Later he posed on the playground as the schoolchildren and teachers behind him raised clenched fists in the air in salute.

On May 15, the science fair was held at Indian Hill School in Grand Blanc. Vicki Weiss's fifth-graders made $50 selling the volcanic ash sent by Truman, and they made plans to send the money to him so he could buy paint for his lodge. Later the students would use the money to buy flowers.

On Friday, May 16, a special Convair 580 scanner plane flew over Mount St. Helens carrying sophisticated computer equipment which took thermal "pictures" of the hot spots on the volcano. The plane returned to its home base near Las Vegas late that evening. A decision was made to wait until Monday to have the data processed by computer technicians to save $1,000 in weekend overtime. Later the thermograph would clearly show that the hot magma was so near the surface that it was melting the ice of the glaciers— an avalanche of the almost cubic-mile bulge was imminent.

On May 17, a motor caravan of 35 Spirit Lake-area property owners, which had been organized by George Bowers and Pauline Lund, was escorted into the Red Zone by officers. The angry and frustrated property owners, some wearing "I've-got-a-piece-of-the-rock" T-shirts, wanted the chance to remove their belongings. Special permission had been granted by Governor Ray—but only after property owners had signed waivers absolving officials of any responsibility.

Skamania sheriff Closner considered the caravan "playing Russian roulette with the mountain" and a State Patrol spotter plane circled over the summit watching for any sign of an eruption. Many of the officers who accompanied the caravan stopped at the lodge to pay courtesy calls on Truman. It was a warm and sunny spring day and they found him in a sport shirt. He had his lawn sprinklers out and running, getting ready for summer. Robert Langdon, superintendent of the Washington State Patrol, stopped by and pointedly offered Truman a trip to "anyplace you want to go." Truman said no thanks. Other law officers who knew Truman better—sheriff Closner and deputy Barker—didn't even bother to ask him.

Shortly before 6 P.M. the officers left, warning Rob Smith and his girlfriend Kathy Paulson that they, too, had to head down the highway in only a few minutes. The two good friends of Truman had been up visiting all afternoon long. They talked about the new culvert they had put in down by Maratta Creek, and their long-postponed plans to clean up Tanglewood Terrace. They agreed they'd have to do that soon.

They were having a hard time parting. Rob and Kathy could sense that Truman didn't want them to leave, that he was reaching out to them. His conversation was thoughtful and sensitive and subdued. Finally Rob and Kathy said they just had to go and Truman followed them over to Rob's black pickup truck. Truman leaned in Rob's window and said he'd see him tomorrow—he was coming to Castle Rock Sunday to buy some bedding plants to start around the lodge, just like Eddie used to do. He grabbed Rob's arm and squeezed it tight and said, "Keep a stiff upper lip, kid."

Rob started up the pickup and they waved goodbye to Truman as they headed down the highway. They were the last people to see Truman alive.

TURN on the news," my sister Dayle shouted over the telephone, "Mount St. Helens has just erupted!"

It was 8:40 A.M. on Sunday, May 18, and I immediately switched on the radio. We quickly decided to skip church so we could listen to the news and find out what had happened to Truman. I remember listening intently to the radio and periodically turning on the TV and flipping the channels to see if there was any film coverage yet.

What news there was was grim. There had been a 5.1 earthquake and the bulge had slid down the mountain in a mighty avalanche. Then there was a cataclysmic explosion, and the volcano's pent-up fury had been unleashed, directly toward Truman's lodge. A report came on the radio: "Spirit Lake has disappeared." I thought, "Oh no!" The worst had happened and it was beyond all comprehension for me.

I rummaged to find the last Christmas card we had received from Truman, as if reading that would somehow mean that he was all right. I found the card, and it had glued to the inside the familiar postcard with the scene of serene Mount St. Helens and Spirit Lake.

Truman had included a note which said:

Glad to hear you and family all O.K.
Bad winter up here so far. Rain – Snow and Wind.
Am doing alright I guess.

Best Wishes
Harry

Then I thought, "He didn't get the letter I sent that told
him I loved him." I had written Truman two letters since
Christmas. By some eerie coincidence, I had mailed each
letter on the day before a major event in Mount St. Helens's
volcanic life. I had sent one on March 19, the day before the
initial earthquake, saying that our 14-year-old son Chris
would like to work at the lake this coming summer, as I had
done at the same age. I sent my second letter to Truman on
Saturday, May 17. I'd had a gnawing feeling about what the
mountain might do and I was worried about Truman's
safety. Yet I also wanted him to know that I understood why
he stayed at the lodge.

The letter was a lengthy one, full of reminiscing. I told
Truman how much I appreciated the summers I had
worked at the lake and how it had had a permanent effect
on my life. I told him I learned so much during those
marvelous summers—not only about him and his life with
Auntie Eddie, but also about myself. I told him how much
fun I'd had then and I teased Truman about my husband
Lee's unsuccessful attempts to buy the pink Cadillac. I told
him that Chris would still like to come up and work there
even though I doubted the authorities would let him open
for business.

I distinctly remember how I ended that letter, because I
knew I had never made the point of saying it or writing it to
him before. I wrote, "I want you to know something, Truman, and that is that I love you."

It was such a special letter—I wanted to be so sure that he
got to read it—that I took it straight to the post office as
soon as I finished it. I remember feeling uneasy as I drove. I
dropped the letter through the slot less than a day before
Truman would be dead.

I couldn't sit and watch what was happening on television. It was all so gruesome, and so many people were suffering. There were massive mudflows and flooding, barren land gray everywhere, and still Mount St. Helens was erupting. I didn't want to think about that, I wanted to remember what it was like when the mountain and Spirit Lake were a paradise in the wilderness. So I went to my room and started to write about Truman. That was fun. He was such a character.

In the days and weeks that followed, newspapers came and I couldn't bring myself to read them or look at any of the pictures. So I'd type another story, trying to recapture the splendor of the most beautiful place I'd ever seen.

I called my sister Dayle and found she felt the same way. We would start reminiscing and our memories would jar more memories loose and we'd laugh together, which felt good. I called my mom, but she was so upset by what had happened she couldn't talk about it.

It was hard to avoid all the news about the eruption. Every day, everywhere I turned there seemed to be something more and I couldn't understand why I was having so much trouble dealing with it. But I kept writing. I was a student at Shoreline Community College in Seattle and I wondered if I could get some class credit for what I was writing. I took some of my Truman stories to Wayne McGuire, my English professor, and he surprised me by saying that they were good, and I should consider writing a book. I decided to give it a try. At the very least our kids would some day enjoy reading what I had written.

As I started out, I became more and more curious about the Truman I didn't know. Truman had never talked with anyone in our family about his past, but after the mountain started stirring he dribbled out bits and pieces to the press. I wanted to know what Truman's friends thought about him and how they felt; I wanted to talk to people who knew Truman when he was young, and what it was like in his early days at Spirit Lake.

I thought of Truman's life as a jigsaw puzzle and I wondered if I could put all the missing pieces together. I knew I had only a few small parts of the puzzle so far. I had known Truman as a man who was always whistling and happy, until Auntie Eddie died. Then his life seemed shrouded in darkness and sadness. I knew Truman as a person who was a bundle of contradictions — kind and mean, sentimental and tough, generous and frugal. Most of all, I knew Truman as a person who loved to be the center of attention. But even that had its contradictions, since he was a private person who let few people penetrate through the wall he had built around himself.

One of the first people I interviewed was Dude Mullooly, who had known Truman when they were both teenagers. She bubbled with enthusiasm and fresh memories from a time 60 years ago. She invited me to her home for lunch and gave me copies of pictures of Truman and her. She was the first person who would be so generous, but far from the last.

I contacted Mossyrock High School and they kindly sent copies of Truman's high school records and the names of people who knew him then. I wrote more letters asking for information, and everyone who responded seemed to send more than just a letter. Ted and Emma Landes sent copies of a 1918 newspaper which had published the letters Truman sent to his mother during World War I. I began to sense how special Truman was to many people, something I had no way of knowing before.

I bought tapes for my tape recorder and drove down to Castle Rock and Longview where I started interviewing people who knew Truman. Everyone kept suggesting other people I should talk with, and the interviews grew to more than 100. I was having a ball. Everyone wanted to share their Truman memories and they were all so nice to me. People continued to give me things — pictures, slides, and poems. The members of the Longview Ski Club even threw a special party so they could show their slides and tell me all about them.

Cathy Douglas, Justice Douglas's widow, wrote three times from Washington, D.C. and gave me information on how to obtain pictures from his personal collection, which had been donated to the Yakima Valley Museum.

I got a letter from Mary Lowry, whose husband Ed had worked with Truman in Chehalis in the early 1920s. She wrote that recently they had met a man named Carl Berg who had visited Truman near the end, and had a long tape of their conversation. I wrote to Carl and he invited me to come listen to it.

I interviewed Carl and his wife Irene at the Toutle Rest Stop on Interstate 5 where they serve free coffee to drivers—one of their services as volunteer members of REACT (Radio Emergency Associated Citizens Teams). Carl had been active helping Cowlitz County monitor the Toutle River ever since Mount St. Helens had first erupted on March 20. Twice a day, Carl would travel into the Red Zone and check the depth gauges on the north and south forks of the Toutle for any possible flooding. He also picked up people who were in the Red Zone illegally and he often stopped to visit Truman.

One April morning, Carl had been checking the river gauges and had picked up a young man named Tom Upchurch who had come a long way in hopes of meeting the now-famous lodge owner. Carl obligingly took Upchurch to meet Truman and he kept his tape recorder going throughout their visit. I sat at the rest stop and listened to that tape for the first of many times with my sister Dayle. Our tears soon flowed. It was just as if Truman was alive and sitting right next to us with the words spilling out so fast you had to know Truman to understand them.

"You tell them down there everything's gone back to normal. The night before last, I got a foot of snow; the night before that, I got a foot of snow. I got 24 inches in 24 hours. You know when you get 24 inches down here, they've got a helluva pile of snow up on the mountain.

"Anything coming out of there—hot or anything, clouds or

dust—that kills it right there. If that had been July or August—you understand in the fall—when there's a run-off of water and the country's all dry and there's no snow, then there's a chance of a washout. But there's not a chance now. You take it at timber line around the side of that hill up there—where the lava ran out a few years ago on the side of that mountain—and there's snow and ice 8 to 12 feet deep and all the gullies have 12 to 15 feet.

"Now, the worst it could do is to pour something down into Dry Gulch, our old washout down there, and fill that up. And then later on sometimes in the spring or summer when it melts, then the whole goddamn road's going to go out again. But I can't foresee any way that the mountain can do a damn thing.

"If it rolled hot lava out, it's not going to go far down that hill because it runs slow. Now glaciers run 60 to 70 miles per hour; they slide down there. But that ice and snow glacier's only comin' down a ways. Hell, they're not coming down any further than timber line.

"I've seen pictures and I don't think much has even come into the Plains of Abraham. It all has to go into the Plains of Abraham and Ape Canyon. It can't come this way. It can't get over that hill! You take that big, rocky jagger right there with no name, all solid rock right there standing in the way. And the Dogs Head up there—that rock that thick—nothing can ever budge that!"

Carl Berg asks: "Tell me now, Harry, as a local—you've been up here 54 years—how does it feel to be a national hero?"

"Oh that's a bunch of hooey, you know. Oh, they're puttin' it on. I didn't want all that. Goddamn it, a lot of people are sayin' ol' Truman did that for publicity, or I done it for financial reasons. I had nothing to do with that and everybody knows I didn't need the goddamn money. I've been closed up.

"I'll tell you what worries me more and this is the goddamn truth. The mountain's never worried me one minute. I knew it wouldn't get me, no earthly way! I wanted to be on the upper side. If it did go out and wash that road all out, I certainly didn't want to be on the lower side. I wanted to be at home in my place where I belong. So I won't budge.

"But I'll tell you, I'm no brave soul. Those earthquakes scared the

hell out of me. They scared the living hell outta me."
Tom Upchurch: "Are you gonna stick it out up here?"
"Oh yeah—hell yeah! I've lived here 54 years. I might as well stay. I'm not leaving my home now. You know, the average people downtown, they don't understand. They think I'm putting on a false front at my place up here. Well, Jesus Christ, I've been here 54 years, I'm going on 84 years old. This is my home.

"I've got a huge spread here—do you realize that? People don't understand. I've got more invested in Spirit Lake financially than the Forest Service, the Y.M.C.A. and all the nesters. You can stack them all in one goddamn big bunch. The money they've got invested won't even touch the 50 acres and my life here. Do you realize that? God, $500,000 wouldn't touch me! I've got more in this goddamn lodge and this one building than three-fourths of them got.

"People don't understand. When you live 54 years in one place and it's the only home you've got, well, you don't just walk off and leave that. Well, Christ no!

"If anything did happen to me, if the mountain did do something, I'd rather go right here with it. If I was down and out of here and lost my home, I wouldn't last a week at my age. I'd just die. I'd have nothing to live for at all and I'd just double up and die. I couldn't make her and everybody knows that. My old heart would stop—if I've got one. A lot of people says I ain't got no heart."

Carl Berg: "By God, you must have one, Harry, to live through these quakes and everything. We'll be back up, Harry. I'm going to have to head back down the road."

"Well, I'm glad you dropped by. You tell everybody down there I'm OK. I thought yesterday I might venture down. I haven't been to town for weeks. I've got a lot of things to do. Of course my neighbors—everybody comes in and brings me food. Smith came in the other day and I sent an order for him. He's coming in again today—young Smith from down below—and he'll bring my groceries and stuff. And of course as far as the liquor is concerned, the media and the newspapers are taking care of that.

"Every damn chopper that comes in brings whiskey in. Now yesterday Field and Stream *was up,* Time *and* Life *was here the day before yesterday. And every magazine and every television and*

radio station in the country have been here. They're all friends of mine.

"*You know, I decided. All through my years, they knew I was ornery and independent. I never let the press print anything, even Ted Natt and the McClellands down in Longview. They never printed anything in their life about me because I wouldn't let them. They've been to my place hundreds of times and wanted to write about it, but I wouldn't do it. No! I wasn't touristy enough. I didn't want to get in any trouble about it. I said they'll dig my life out.*

"*But three or four weeks ago, one morning I decided. I thought, Hell, I'm an old man. I said, hell, I'll make up to them. And I have, I've made up with every newspaper, every television, every radio in the United States of America.*

"*They've come in and I've poured them a drink, I've poured them a Coke. They've lived with me and I've made a solid friend of every one of them. If anybody ever had the nerve to say anything about Harry Truman, every newspaper, every radio, and every television would be on their back tomorrow — wouldn't they?*

"*I done that intentionally. I made friends of the whole goddamn bunch. Because I'll tell you, the press is all-powerful. They are so powerful I'd rather have them on my side 100 percent.*"

Carl Berg: "I bet you'll have a good tourist trade coming up this summer."

"*Well, that's what I'm worried about. I don't want it, goddamn it! I don't want them to come back. I'll have to put a crew in here; I'll have to open my cocktail lounge and restaurant. I'll have to put two boys on the float; I'll have to put two girls in the goddamn cabins.*

"*You know, I'm retired. I've done no merchandising or commercializing for several years. I closed my restaurant and closed this lodge. I rent my cabins and rent my boats — just what I can run myself the last two or three years. It keeps me busier than hell doin' that. I'm an old man.*

"*But Jesus Christ, now with that bunch of cabins and 100 boats and all those motors and my launch and that cocktail lounge and restaurant sittin' there and this building asittin' here, it scares the hell out of me. I just hope and I believe it will — I think the bubble will bust and they're forgettin' the damn thing now. I just hope when spring comes and this thing opens up, they'll still forget it. Because, God, that'd be a mess if I have to go back in business at my age."*

Carl Berg: "We have to back down the hill."

"OK, kid, tell everybody that I'm OK, that I'm fine and not to worry about me. I'm doin' fine; I've got everything I need. Now this is true, I'm not braggin' a bit.

"Nothing can happen in a minute that there wouldn't be 10 'copters in here to get ol' Truman out. They'd be right here; they're right here day and night. The other day I had four right here lined up in the road at one time—from around the country.

"Jesus Christ! The state knows I'm here, the government knows I'm here, everybody knows I'm here. Why, if anything happened and any emergency came, there'd be the goddamnedest line of 'copters sittin' out here you'd ever saw. This area would be full of 'copters comin' to get ol' Truman, wouldn't they? They'd jerk me off here in three minutes—you know that."

The tape stopped and I was filled with conflicting feelings. Truman's voice was so alive that I just couldn't believe he was really dead. And I kept thinking how much I now wished I had taken the time to get to know him better. But I knew he never invited that kind of closeness and when I was with him, I somehow didn't feel quite welcome after Auntie Eddie died. The worst thing of all was the haunting thought that I would like to have gone with my sister Elaine when she visited Truman on May 1. Maybe then I could have told him what I wrote in that letter he never received.

On June 14, there was a memorial service for Truman at the American Baptist Church in Longview. It was less than a month after the eruption and I felt the service was being held too soon. I wanted to cling to the faint glimmer of hope that Truman somehow might still be alive, that he had made it to his secret "hidey hole" stocked with Schenley's, as he always boasted he would. The memorial service made it all seem too final.

It was the day after another of Mount St. Helens's secondary eruptions, but the church was filled. There were many of Truman's old friends—George Barker, George

Bowers, the Quoidbachs and Jim Lund. John Garrity and
Doc Peterson had come from Minnesota. There were many
of the reporters who had considered Truman a friend as
well as a great story. There were people I had never seen
before.

And there were flowers, including the basket bought with
the money sent by Vicki Weiss's fifth-graders in Grand
Blanc, Michigan. After Truman had died, there were many
tears and broken hearts in that classroom, and the students
had decided to do something to commemorate their special
friendship with Truman. A local company had supplied a
memorial stone and it was placed in a quiet corner of the
school grounds. The inscription reads:

HARRY TRUMAN

Born October 20, 1896
Died May 18, 1980
A Man With Great Courage
Who Would Not Leave His Mountain.
May His Spirit Live On.

The message at the memorial service in Longview was
delivered by Dr. Richard Ice, president of American Baptist
Homes in Oakland, California. He had known Truman
since he was a child and he recalled how Truman had
written on a Christmas card that he just couldn't understand how God could take Auntie Eddie away from him.

"So Harry didn't understand God—which may not have
upset God too much," Dr. Ice said. "And perhaps God didn't
fully understand Harry Truman, either. But no one lives his
life amidst the incredible beauty of Spirit Lake and Mount
St. Helens without a deep theism we could not likely define.
Harry was a man of the seasons—he didn't resist nature, he
respected it—and he was a creature of the cycles nature
brings. Wherever Harry is now, he's taking charge of the
situation around him. If he can see what's going on here,
he's saying, 'Don't you dare cry about me! I did just what I
wanted. Go have a good time!'"

I was still having trouble looking at pictures and books about Mount St. Helens. But that was slowly changing as I talked to more and more people and found that many shared the same feelings.

On September 13, there was to be an auction to dispose of Truman's personal possessions left at Prindle. Initially I thought the auction was a good idea, especially since our family was going to be given the chance to buy a few things the day before the auction; my mom and aunt had inherited half of Truman's estate. We were particularly interested in the picture of Grandma's home in Sweden, which we thought was still there.

My two sisters, my two cousins, my mother and I all drove down to Prindle from Seattle. But as soon as we arrived, our disappointments began. We found the Prindle residence run down, overgrown by brambles, and sadly deteriorated, not at all the way we remembered it when Auntie Eddie was alive. And we also found that all but one or two of Auntie Eddie's personal possessions had already been removed, including the picture of grandma's home.

Preparations for the auction seemed like a ghoulish circus and made me sick to my stomach. I knew it would be even worse on auction day and it all reminded me of Truman's comment to a couple of his friends that "there will be vultures flying around waiting to clean up after I die." Neither my mother nor I could force ourselves to go to the auction. But several other members of the family did and that night on the network news we saw my sister Elaine paying $160 for a milk pitcher with a broken spout that had been in our family for almost 100 years.

On the day of the auction, I wanted to recapture more memories of Truman so I spent the day interviewing. That day, I met Jim Lund, a marvelous funny man with a jade tooth. I decided to stay an extra day so I could do more interviews. My sister Dayle and I had driven up the Spirit Lake Highway to the barricades across the road and the signs that said:

RED ZONE   RED ZONE
Extreme Hazard   Hazard Area
AREA CLOSED   Entry Beyond
To Public   This Point
                            By Permit Only

Along the way up the highway, we had seen the ravaged Toutle River and I was astounded by what I saw. But many of the people I had interviewed had flown over the devastated Red Zone and they said it was something I should see. I was caught in a tug-of-war with my emotions. How would I handle such an experience? Wouldn't it give me perspective I needed for my writing?

On Monday, September 15, my sister Elaine and I started back to Seattle. We had stopped along the way, and for the first time I had been able to buy a volcano book and look through it. It was a beautiful fall day, with clear skies and bright sunshine, and we both said simultaneously, "Let's do it, let's take a flight today."

So we drove east to the tiny airport at Toledo, which had been the scene of so much activity when the rescue efforts were mounted May 18. We drove up to the small cedar-shake shack with the sign that said Rocky's Volcano Flights. Rocky Kilberg, the owner, greeted us and said the $25 flights lasted about 45 minutes and there would be about a 30-minute wait. He had three pilots on duty that day and he added our name to the blackboard waiting list. He decided to take us up himself in his small green-and-white Cessna 172.

It was beautiful when we took off and I was immediately glad we had decided to do it. I looked below at the patchwork of green and golden fields and the jade-colored trees—a lovely tapestry as the Cowlitz River wove its way through the farms and towns in the valley. The plane seemed to hang motionless in the air.

But suddenly the landscape changed. The green forests turned a rusty brown—thousands of acres affected by the

eruption of Mount St. Helens. Then we flew over vast areas
where all the trees had been blown down, stripped of
branches and bark, all gray and looking like pick-up sticks.
There was not a hint of green anywhere. I couldn't com-
prehend the massiveness of the devastation. Later I would
learn that 150 square miles of timber were blown down.

We flew over the logging roads that had snaked over the
mountainous terrain, where huge logging trucks and heavy
equipment looked like toys tossed aside by children. We flew
over Forest Lake, Elk Lake and Haniford Lake. The water
had been blown out of them, and what remained looked like
dark brown mud puddles.

We flew over the Mount Margaret back country where
Auntie Eddie and I had so enjoyed our day-long hike together and the lovely meadow where we had sat eating
ham-and-cheese sandwiches. There was nothing to remind
me of what once was there; the hills were naked and everything was an unrelenting mud-gray. I thought of it as the
color of death and suddenly I started crying.

I couldn't hold back the tears and they streamed down my
face as I looked at a nightmare world made real. Rocky was
yelling over the chugging of the engine and it was hard to
understand what he was saying. I felt as if I was in a foggy
daze. I was vaguely aware of the smell of sulphur as we flew
over Bear Pass and on to the north end of what had once
been beautiful Spirit Lake. It was now a brown cesspool
dotted with pulverized debris. I could only guess where
Truman's lodge once was.

I couldn't quit crying, so I tried to think of something
happy. I thought of Jim Lund and all the crazy, funny
stories he had told me about Truman and how he told me,
"That old sinner was just a hell-bound sinner. But he's not
going to hades. He maybe won't end up in paradise either.
He'll find some middle ground, and he'll smuggle whiskey
one way and ice and mixer the other. God, I loved that guy."

And I thought about Truman's friend Rob Smith, who
had come to mean so much to him after Auntie Eddie died,

and how he and Truman had plans to steal "that whole damn Forest Service rock pile."

My mind snapped back from those memories as Rocky yelled and pointed to where Harmony Falls once was. The beautiful waterfall was gone. All that was left was a little slope colored an ugly brown.

Rocky pointed to where he thought Truman's lodge had been and I could suddenly hear Truman's words on that tape: "Spirit Lake and Mount St. Helens are part of me—they're mine—they're as much a part of me as my arms and legs. If I left the mountain and the lake, I'd just fold up and die."

It all looked so violent, and I wondered why Truman had once told John Garrity that he wanted to die a violent death. I was torn—he had obviously gone the way he would have wanted, with all his precious possessions and the lodge he loved—but it was all so awful and awesomely sad. I tried to concentrate on what I believe—that death is only sad for those who are left.

But I couldn't. I glanced up at the hellish gouge in Mount St. Helens which had rained death, devastation, and 400 million tons of earth into the atmosphere.

The plane ride lasted another 15 minutes or so, but I don't remember anything else I saw. All I remember is a terrible ache and continuing to cry.